THE Gibson L5

Its History and its Players

by ADRIAN INGRAM

Foreward by Bob Benedetto

ISBN 1-57424-047-1
SAN 683-8022

Cover art & color design by Jim Filippi

1940 L5P with Gibson amp and matching guitar case

THE Gibson L5

Its History and its Players

by ADRIAN INGRAM

CONTENTS

APPENDICES

Photo: Dennis Trantham

Jimmy Stewart playing his 1984 L5-CES/L5 custom

FOREWORD

As a youngster, guitars were all I ever thought about. I played guitar on weekends in a local band and in bed at night, I'd pour over guitar catalogs — mostly Gibson's—and recall knowing exactly which archtop model and its endorsers were on each page. Because I had few other interests to distract me, I studied those catalogs. The L-5 of course was *the* guitar.

Precursor of the modern archtop guitar, the groundbreaking L-5 was added to the Gibson Guitar Company's product line in late 1922. An immediate and overwhelming success, it turned the heads of makers, players and listeners alike. The first archtop guitar to feature f-holes, it was designed to project through the horn-dominated bands of the day. Its strong, full and warm sound was the ideal marriage with the piano and bass. Replacing the banjo, it was the perfect orchestral rhythm instrument.

Gibson didn't stop with the acoustic L-5. As the potential of its well-balanced voice became apparent, Gibson pushed the L-5 to the forefront by introducing the amplified CES model. Now, a *solo* instrument! The impact on jazz guitar was monumental and lasting. From early jazz guitar pioneers such as Eddie Lang to modern players like Tuck Andress, the L-5 proved itself to be the quintessential jazz guitar.

It is indisputably the basis for all other archtops, whether mass-produced or the product of individual makers. While most makers strive for innovative success, originality in form and function is not easily attained. Though refinements have certainly been made to the f-hole guitar design over the last 75 years, the L-5 established the standard .

It has always been, and no doubt always will be, an inspiration and benchmark for all to follow. As a maker of archtop guitars, I am a proponent of the company that has spent more R&D time than any other manufacturer/maker developing the most popular jazz guitar in the world. I know of no makers, players, dealers or collectors who are unaware of the L-5's impact on the guitar community.

With the archtop guitar's evergrowing popularity, it seems fitting that there be a book honoring the one model which started it all. A scholar as well as a professional guitarist for over 30 years, author Adrian Ingram is a respected and prolific writer, having penned 15 guitar books ranging from the instructional to the biographical. Intimately knowledgeable on the construction of the instrument as well as the music performed on it, jazz guitar is his passion.

What then could be more appropriate than this tribute to the world's most popular jazz guitar, written by one of jazz guitar's most gifted players as well as its foremost historian.

I tip my hat to both!

ROBERT BENEDETTO

Photo courtesy Craig Brody, The Guitar Broker, Ft. Lauderdale, Florida

Bob Benedetto with a 1961 L-5C (Electric Special) #16679.

1963 George Gobel CES

This book is dedicated to Ed Benson without whose generous help and expertise it would not have been possible.

Adrian Ingram

1948 L5P

ACKNOWLEDGEMENTS

Joe Bawelino, Bob Benedetto, Ed Benson, Adrian Bevis, Bob Bozzo, Joshua Breakstone, Chris Burden, Royce Campbell, Walter Carter, Max Davidson, Don DeMarco, Heiner Franz, Hank Garland, Marty Grosz, Richie Hart, Richard Head (Gibson Corp.), Hutch Hutchings (Gibson Corp.), June Ingram, Lucy Ingram, Ike Isaacs, Stanley Jay (Mandolin Brothers), Paul Johnson (Gruhn Guitars), Just Jazz Guitar, Jeane Pierre Llabador, Peter Leitch, Mundell Lowe, Jack Machechnie, Ian MacGregor, Pat Martino, Lou Mecca, Ron Moore, Van Moretti, Tony Mottola, Trefor Owen, Bob Ragozinno, Jim Rowen, Roy Sainsbury, Alexander Schmitz, Michael Serota, Tim Shaw, Louis Stewart, Tom Van Hoose, Larry Wexer, Danny Weber, Jack Wilkins, Robert Yelin,

Django Reinhardt try's an L5 with DeArmond pickup in 1949

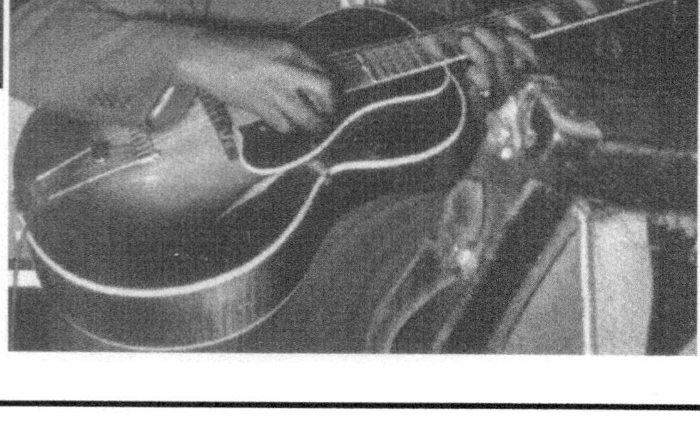

Al Casey, from the Louis Armstrong band, also plugs in a L5 in 1941

Louis Stewart and Heiner Franz duet on a modified ES150 and a 1970's L5CESN

A 1963 L5CES and its stablemate the Super 400 CES

CHAPTER 1

Origins

ORVILLE GIBSON

Orville Gibson

Orville Gibson was born in Chateaugay, New York in 1856. By the 1870s his family had moved to Kalamazoo and Orville was working as a clerk in a shoe store, pursuing at the same time, a passionate interest in woodwork and the construction of stringed instruments. This apparently all-consuming hobby, enabled him to develop and refine his woodworking skills to such a degree that he was soon able to carve mandolins and violins of the highest quality. Yet with only the most basic tools, and a limited 10 x 12 woodworking shop, Orville could not meet the increasing demand for his instruments. So heavy was this demand, that on October 11th 1902 a group of enterprising businessman took the, retrospectively monumental, step of incorporating the GIBSON MANDOLIN – GUITAR manufacturing company.

Having met with this undoubted "commercial" success, Orville soon lost interest in the day to day manufacturing process. While he found the business side of the company onerous, he nevertheless maintained an active interest in design, acoustics and performance. Up until his death on August 19, 1918, his role within the company had in effect changed from manager to consultant.

The precepts upon which Orville Gibson's first mandolins were based–namely that the most effective and efficient vibrations were found in unbent and unstressed carved wood, were adopted wholeheartedly by the fledgling company. An accomplished guitar player, Orville Gibson was much in demand as an accompanist. It was only a matter of time, therefore, before he applied his radical ideas to the construction of guitars.

How would you like

---an instrument built as Stradivarius built his violins

This construction used on Gibson Mandolins, Mandolas, Mando-cellos, Mando-bass, Guitars and Harp-Guitars

Sounding Board and Back Board cut from a solid block

---and graduated to retain all the vibratory sensitiveness

A GIBSON TOP

After completion of the first carving (upper side), the under side is carved, and the top then passes through hundreds of operations before it is ready for its important part in a finished Gibson

STRADIVARIUS was among the first to develop the graduated sounding board and back board which so vitally influences beauty of tone and vibratory sensitiveness.

He carved out the fronts and backs from a solid block of wood just as Gibson is doing it today, instead of bending to shape from a flat piece. These boards are carefully graduated by hand from a certain thickness at the center to a delicate thinness near the outer edge, and this, to a great degree, accounts for the wonderful tonal qualities of Gibson Instruments.

This delicate graduation leaves the grain layers and fibers in their natural position, free and sensitive, helping to amplify vibrations to their finest possibilities.

The selection of materials for these sounding boards permits of no slighting of quality. Only the finest grade of spruce is used, as nearly white as it is possible to obtain, of firm texture with long, straight, close grain. Painstaking care is taken in its selection by artisans who, after years of experience, know Gibson requirements.

Back boards are made only from the finest quality of straight or curly grained hard Northern Michigan Maple, depending on the style and grade of the instrument.

The faithfulness of reproduction in Gibson Instruments and their increasing mellowness of tone as the years go by is only possible because of the construction and material put into these sounding boards, backs and rims.

Between 1904 and 1924, the heyday of the large mandolin orchestras, Gibson produced what many consider to be amongst the finest mandolins ever made. Similarly, the round–hole arched top guitars, produced during the same period, established the precedent, not only for Gibson's L5, but also for the work of such fine luthiers as John D'Angelico, Elmer Stromberg and Epi Stathopoulo (Epiphone guitars).

In fact Orville Gibson's belief that the gourd shaped carved top design was superior, to the then contemporaneous flat topped or ribbed mandolins and guitars, quickly became the pervasive influence in guitar manufacture. Even though Lloyd Loar was later to further refine Gibson's ideas, the archtop guitar had nonetheless arrived!

early oval hole Gibson archtop

As the sales of mandolins and guitars increased still further, the company outgrew its premises on several occasions. In fact it relocated no less than four times before opening its now famous factory at 225 Parsons Street, Kalamazoo. This location was situated in the centre of the so-called "furniture belt" of Western Michigan, with access to a pool of highly skilled craftsmen, as well as the latest developments in woodworking machinery. In no less than 10 years after its incorporation, Gibson had become the largest institution in the world devoted exclusively to the manufacture of high quality fretted instruments.

The Gibson plant at 225 Parson's street

Lloyd Loar

Although Orville Gibson produced the first archtop guitars, using carved tops similar to those found on violins and 'cellos, it was in fact Lloyd Loar who was responsible for Gibsons' adoption of violin type "F" holes. The resulting instruments owed as much in appearance to the cello, as to their fretted predecessors, and have, as a result, since been generically described as "cello style" guitars.

Loar, who held a Master of Music degree, was a virtuoso mandolinist, composer and an acoustical engineer of high repute. His combined musical knowledge and acoustic engineering skills enabled him to make an enormous contribution to the design and development of Gibson's ever expanding range of fretted instruments.

Amongst the components he designed or improved were the adjustable bridge, elevated pickguards and banjo mutes. His refinements to Orville Gibson's carved bodied instruments resulted in the model F5 mandolin and the L5 guitar. These not only had tap tuned carved tops and backs, but also the first "F" holes found on any fretted instruments since the Baroque period (circa 1650-1750).

As the mandolin was Loar's speciality, it was hardly surprising that this instrument was the first to receive the "violin" style 'F' holes. The model in question, appropriately designated the F5, was in many ways the direct antecedent of the L5 guitar, which was later to adopt several of the F5's distinctive features.

model F5 mandolin

From the outset Gibson recycled its most successful design features; combining them, in a variety of ways, in the production of new models. Carved tops, raised pickguards, adjustable bridges and 'f' holes were but a few of the features which quickly migrated from one instrument to another.

In retrospect it is clear that Loar's brilliantly conceived mandolin became the catalyst for many of the standard features found on Gibson's later mandolins and archtop guitars. Parallel top braces, maple necks, the bound tortoiseshell pickguard with right angled support, and the newly-patented truss rod, under a fretboard raised clear of the carved top, were perhaps the most obvious features to be carried across from the F5 to Gibson's expanding range of archtop guitars.

The L5 guitar was appropriately afforded a similar hierarchical position in the company's growing range and in so doing acquired the F5's exquisite ornamentation; notably the multiple bindings and peghead flowerpot inlays. In keeping with Gibson's tendency to recycle, the flowerpot inlay transferred blatantly from the F5 to the L5 was, in itself, a further refinement of a pattern previously found on the F4 mandolin, H4 mandola and K4 mandocello.

flowerpot peghead inlay of the F5 mandolin

The F5 was introduced in June 1922, and predated the first L5 by several months. Understandably, both instruments went on to become "classics" of their kind, although the L5 was to later undergo further refinements, relating to size, construction and ornamentation.

The first L5s were made towards the close of 1922, and in the hands of players like Eddie Lang, George M Smith, Nick Lucas and Roy Smeck, were soon to play an important role in the, "dance orchestras" of the period.

The Embassy Club Orchestra: (L to R) Eddie Lang, Tommy Dorsey, Fuzzy Farrar, Al Duffy, Stan King, Jimmy Dorsey, and Arthur Schutt, an all star band.

Throughout the 1920s, Loar perfected a new method of construction for the Mastertone banjo (a floating head, with ball bearing rim and central tone tube) as well as the design for several other "Master" instruments including the now defunct tenor lute and mando-'cello. His piece de resistance, however, (excepting of course, the L5 and F5), was the conception and development of an electric bass. Prophetically anticipating demand by almost 30 years, Loar's iconoclastic vision was snubbed by Gibson; a rebuff which ultimately led to Loar's resignation in 1924. Furthermore, this was not the first and would not be the last occasion when Gibson's engineers were far ahead of their time. We shouldn't forget that Orville Gibson created the company in the first instance to pursue the development of his futuristic innovations in fretted instrument lutherie. Mercifully, he was not thwarted by company beaurocracy. Lloyd Loar lost control, and was totally demoralized by the inertia which so often surrounds the infrastructure of boards and committees which inevitably spring up as a company increases in size.

Nevertheless, by the time Loar had left Gibson, the synthesis of violin family acoustics and the construction of fretted instruments was well established. The basic principles behind this successful marriage of ideas may be summarized as

1) a carved, graduated top and back,
2) a tilted angle of attachment for the neck, and concomitant high, but adjustable bridge.
3) the violin type 'f' holes and
4) the use of a metal tailpiece to secure the strings and increase sustain.

Lloyd Loar's **MASTER GUITAR–the L5 Professional Special Grand Concert Model,** to give it its full title, was the first guitar to successfully utilize all of the aforementioned features, and thus become that catalyst for Gibson's entire post 1923 range of archtop guitars.

Eddie Lang, real name Salvatore Massaro. In 1931 he was at the top of his career and was regarded world-wide as 'the jazz guitarist", playing his Gibson L5

The L5 typified Gibson's innovative marriage of violin acoustics and fretted instrument construction.

The Carter family from Virginia included Maybelle on an early Gibson L5, Sara on the autoharp and A.P. Carter.

CHAPTER 2

Sweet Sixteen

THE L5 - 1923 TO 1924

It should be stressed at the outset that it is impossible to date precisely the changes of cosmetic features and upgrades in components. Such changes were gradual and generally random, particularly in the early stages. Unless confirmed by accurate data such as Shipping Totals, blueprints or patents, the dates have been determined by hands-on experience and contemporaneous literature. Even from the same shipment, no two L5s were totally identical.

The L5 acquired its suffix simply because it was the company's fifth production line archtop. Although it was preceded by the L1 (1902-1925), L2 (1902-1926), L3 (1902-1933), and , and L4 (1912-1956), it was the first archtop guitar to utilize Lloyd Loar's "F" hole design. Moreover it's silver plated metal parts (gold from 1924), triple bound peghead with ornate flowerpot inlay and triple A grade timbers, set it apart from all of the company's previous guitars.

In short the L5 was Gibson's flagship; a luxury guitar which over a relatively short period replaced the tenor banjo as a rhythm instrument and provided the basis for the company's undisputed dominance in the field of archtop manufacture. It established a standard for archtop guitar manufacture which other corporate manufacturing companies and individual luthiers were soon to be measured by. The first version of the L5 was manufactured between 1922 and 1924. Its simple, yet decorative appointments belied the quality of construction and timbers. Its 16" body width and 24 3/4" scale were borrowed from the L4, as was the decorative point at the end of the ebony fingerboard (this particular feature was also used on the 1906/7 Style 'O' guitar). Simple pearl dots were used as position markers on frets 5, 7, 9, 12 (2 dots) and 15.

Marty Grosz with 16" dot marker L5

The top was carved from two pieces of spruce, while the back and sides were bookmatched maple, although some of the earliest L5s used birch instead of maple. The carefully selected tops and backs were tap tuned and then ornamented by triple white and black binding. Similar binding was also used for the peghead veneer, which was originally the most overtly decorative part of the instrument.

The art nouveau flowerpot inlay, first used in a similar form on the headstock of the 1911 F4 mandolin, was inlaid into the L5's peghead veneer directly below the company logo. On the first variant L5 the logo (The Gibson) was sited diagonally between the D and G tuning pegs as opposed to the later practice of siting it horizontally above them.

A black plastic, bell shaped, cover completed the headstock appointments. Situated approximately half an inch above the nut, this cover provided a clever way of hiding the routing at the end of the truss rod channel, whilst at the same time allowing access to the tensioning nut. The truss rod itself was patented by Thaddeus McHugh in 1921. Simple in concept, though somewhat limited in action, this curved steel rod sat in a narrow channel (beneath the fingerboard) which ran horizontally between the headstock and heel of the neck. It served to reinforce the laminated timbers and balance the tension of the strings, thereby keeping the neck in perfect alignment.

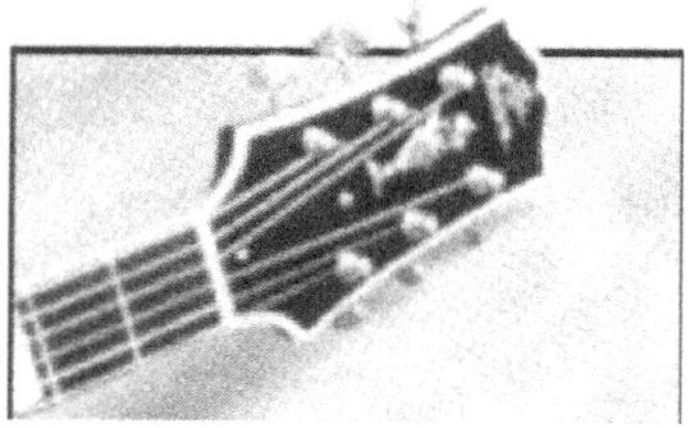

closeup of L5 truss rod cover

On account of their hierarchical position, L5s were amongst the first instruments to use the newly patented truss rod. Following the expiry of its patent, however, McHugh's truss rod became a standard fitting on the majority of steel string guitars produced by rival companies.

The L5's elongated celluloid pickguard was pinned to the side of the neck, and affixed to the rim of the body via an adjustable (screw threaded) metal rod and 'foot' which was attached to the pickguard by a plastic 'riser-block'. The pickguard was unbound throughout the instrument's first year of production, but later acquired 3 ply binding more in keeping with the ornamentation of the body and headstock.

Many of the earliest L5s were fitted with a novel device called the Virzi Tone-Producer. Fundamentally a second sound-board suspended from the inside top of the guitar, this small oval gizmo was reputed to increase the instruments volume and projection. Gibson's engineers, however, were not convinced and appear to have had little faith in this unproven device; consequently it was discontinued after Loar's resignation. Even while Loar was at Gibson, a number of L5s were produced without it. Furthermore, many early instruments have since had their Virzi's removed and it is nowadays rare to find an L5 with this device intact.

While the 1922/4 L5 embodied many of the features found on its various descendants, the Virzi Tone-Producer, unbound pickguard and birch back, set it apart from later models, as did the dual labeling system devised to show Loar's involvement and approval of Gibson's 'Master' range models.

Up until 1924 there were two labels attached to the inside of the body: the "Gibson Master Model" label used for all Style '5' instruments and a second label which read:

'The top, back, tonebars and airchamber of this instrument were tested, tuned, and the assembled instrument tried and approved (the date), Lloyd Loar, Acoustical Engineer"

The model designation, serial number, date and Loar's signature were hand written. This additional label was discontinued towards the end of 1924 after Loar's resignation, but the original Master Model label continued to be used up until 1929. Nevertheless, the company's use of these labels had always been erratic; for example not every Lloyd Loar L5 carried the second label, and even the Master Model label itself was used randomly between 1927 and 1929.

The 2nd Variant L5 - 1925 to 1930

Several significant changes were made to the L5 following the departure of Lloyd Loar. Understandably, the label bearing his signature, and personal endorsement of the Master Range, was discontinued. So too was the Virzi Tone-Producer; a gizmo of which the company's directors and acoustical engineers had always been skeptical.

A little later, the ornately engraved silver plated machine heads, (with mother-of-pearl buttons), were also changed, from individual tuners to pegs which were mounted side by side on a metal strip. These were made by Waverly, a company previously used by Gibson for their high quality mandolin fittings.

Other changes to the headstock included the resiting of the company logo above the 4th and 3rd string tuners. Furthermore, the logo was inlaid into the peghead veneer horizontally rather than diagonally, as had been the practice up until this point.

The peghead logo sited horizontally on the second variant L5

Necks continued to be made from two bookmatched blocks of maple with a central mahogany strip. The ebony fingerboard gained an extra position marker at the third fret, around the same time as the company logo in the peghead was resited (circa 1927).

For reasons long forgotten, the decorative point at the end of the fingerboard was dropped in the summer of 1929 and not used again until the mid-thirties.

By 1930 the L5 had become the premier steel string guitar of its time, played and endorsed by the likes of Nick Lucas, Eddie Lang, Maybelle Carter, Harry Volpe, and Snoozer Quinn.

The 3rd Variant L5 - 1930 to 1937

The 16 inch body L5 underwent its most significant changes between 1930 and 1934. Many of the resulting features were later transferred to the "advanced" 17 inch L5 (introduced in 1934), which was soon to replace its smaller cousin. Consequently, the 3rd variant provided an important link between the earliest L5 and the L5 as we know it today.

Perhaps the most distinctive change lay in the new position markers, which were upgraded from simple dots to wide pearloid blocks. In keeping with those found on the 2nd variant, the markers started at the 3rd fret and were repeated at frets 5, 7, 9, 12 and 15. By 1934, and corresponding with the introduction of the larger "advanced" body L5, the decorative point at the end of the fingerboard was also reinstated.

Other cosmetic changes included a modernized company logo which stated simply, yet boldly, "Gibson" instead of "The Gibson" which had appeared on the earlier models .

Towards the close of 1930, individual open-backed, Grover machineheads replaced those supplied by Waverly, and were used up until the introduction of Klusons.

The third variant L5 can be further differentiated from its predecessors by its longer pickguard. This was screwed directly into the top of the guitar as opposed to using the complicated neck pinning system found on earlier models. A non-compensated ebony bridge, of greater bulk, was also introduced, although this was used randomly, as many L5s continued to utilize the compensated rosewood version found on earlier models.

Between 1934 and 1937 the 16 inch L5 was gradually phased out. The introduction of a bigger and louder instrument saw the relegation of 16 inch bodies to instruments lower down the range such as the L48 (1946-1971), the L50 (1934-1971) and the L75 (1934-1939).

There was a period of 3 years when the final version of the 16" L5 and the advanced 17" model co-existed. But the writing was on the wall. Between 1935 and 1937, its final year of production, only 99 16" models were produced as compared to 200 with the larger body.

Third variant of L5 with Block markers

1936 Gibson catalogue

MASTER MODEL GUITAR

STYLE L-5

The King of all guitars—a thousand dollars couldn't build a guitar with a finer tone. A tone that satisfies—listen for quality—it's there; listen for power—it's there; listen for clearness and balance, and you'll find it in this guitar.

The finest of materials—the finest of craftsmen—the finest of equipment, is used in building the Master Guitar; that is why artists say "I play an L-5" instead of just saying "I play a guitar".

FEATURES

WOOD: Highly figured curly maple back, rim and neck; finest Adirondack spruce top; ebony fingerboard.

FINISH AND DECORATIONS: Rich Cremona brown with golden sunburst on top, rims, back and neck. Top and bottom of rim and sides of neck bound with white, black, white ivoroid. Large pearloid position marks; pearl peghead inlays.

FITTINGS: Individual machine heads; adjustable bridge; extension tailpiece; elevated fingerrest; gold plated metal parts.

BODY SIZE: Grand concert; 16" wide and 20" long.

PRICE: $275.00.

See page 48 for cases.

NO BENDING

NO HEATING

NO SOAKING

NO VENEERS

STYLE L-5
$275.00

1933 Master Model from early Gibson catalog

The L-5

Today, as for many years, the L-5 is an exceedingly popular orchestra guitar—the choice of the most critical artists. Those who value consistent peak performance and full, melodious tone, know the L-5 is a dependable and worthy partner.

Of the finest selected spruce, curly maple and rosewood, the L-5 is 17″ wide and 21″ long and has a non-vibrating gold and silver tailpiece richly engraved, and burnished with matching "Sealfast" individual machine heads.

The pearl inlaid fingerboard, Vari-Tone control, ivoroid binding and the adjustable Truss Rod are all exclusive Gibson features of the L-5 which is available in gleaming Natural Finish or the traditional Cremona brown with golden sunburst shading.

The L-5 may also be had in the Cut-Away style.

L-5 Guitar—Regular Finish
L-5N Guitar—Natural Finish
L-5C Cut-Away Guitar—Regular Finish
L-5CN Cut-Away Guitar—Natural Finish

Cases for Above Instruments

609 *Challenge* 606 *Faultless* 600 *Faultless*

There was a period of 3 years when the advanced 17" L5 (shown above) and the 16" L5 were both produced at the same time.

CHAPTER 3

Advancing The Cause

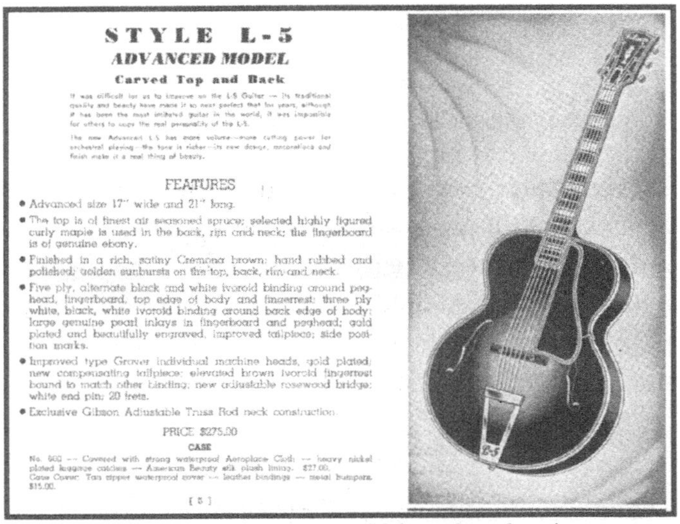

STYLE L-5
ADVANCED MODEL
Carved Top and Back

It was difficult for us to improve on the L-5 Guitar — its traditional quality and beauty have made it so near perfect that for years, although it has been the most imitated guitar in the world, it was impossible for others to copy the real personality of the L-5.

The new Advanced L-5 has more volume—more cutting power for orchestral playing—the tone is richer—its new design, decorations and finish make it a real thing of beauty.

FEATURES

- Advanced size 17" wide and 21" long.
- The top is of finest air seasoned spruce; selected highly figured curly maple is used in the back, rim and neck; the fingerboard is of genuine ebony.
- Finished in a rich, satiny Cremona brown; hand rubbed and polished; golden sunbursts on the top, back, rim and neck.
- Five ply, alternate black and white ivoroid binding around peghead, fingerboard, top edge of body and fingerrest; three ply white, black, white ivoroid binding around back edge of body; large genuine pearl inlays in fingerboard and peghead; gold plated and beautifully engraved, improved tailpiece; side position marks.
- Improved type Grover individual machine heads, gold plated; new compensating tailpiece; elevated brown ivoroid fingerrest bound to match other binding; new adjustable rosewood bridge; white end pin; 20 frets.
- Exclusive Gibson Adjustable Truss Rod neck construction.

PRICE $275.00

CASE

No. 600 — Covered with strong waterproof Aeroplane Cloth — heavy nickel plated luggage catches — American Beauty silk plush lining. $27.00.
Case Cover: Tan zipper waterproof cover — leather bindings — metal bumpers. $15.00.

[5]

Page 5 from Gibson's 1936 catalog showing the Style L5 - Advanced Model.

The popularity of Gibson's "F" hole archtop guitar was clear from the outset. Although in 1930 there was only one "F" hole archtop in the entire Gibson range, by 1935 there were nine (excluding tenor guitars). Much of the impetus for this rapid expansion came from the unprecedented growth of rival companies such as Epiphone and Gretsch. Harmony also introduced a number of F hole archtop guitars in 1933, with a view to capturing the lower end of the market. Of these rival companies, Epiphone was by far the greatest threat; their introduction of a full range of "Masterbuilt" archtops in 1931 virtually compelled Gibson to make a similar response. Indeed, the following 2 decades evidenced great rivalry between Gibson and Epiphone and, for that matter, the players who appear to have been tenaciously loyal to their chosen brand. In 1934, Epiphone's top models: the DeLuxe, Tudor and Broadway were, at 16 3/8", marginally wider than the L5. That same year, Gibson was to start what eventually turned into a "battle of the widths", with the launch of its 18" bodied Super 400.

cover of Epiphone's 1934 catalog

Following this monumental step, Gibson continued its "bigger is better" campaign by revamping the majority of its archtops; advancing the width of their bodies from 16" to 17" and from 14 3/4" to 16". It was at this point that the company began its policy of filling out the range both above and below its standard models and two new 14 3/4" width guitars were also introduced to slot beneath the L5O.

The "Super 400"

The choicest of the finest materials the world has to offer—workmanship such as can come only with a quarter of a century of experience—infinite care in making and matching every single part, whether it is an entire back or a small piece of bracing—inlay and binding that is pure artistry—heavy gold plating and engraving — a beautiful hand rubbed and shaded finish that completes this picture of perfection. And of course, the tone, voicing and power that only the combination of these integral parts can produce.

Gibson 1936 catalog featuring the 18" Super 400

Construction

With the larger bodied guitars came substantial alteration, both in methods of construction and styles of ornamentation. In order to adequately support the larger top, the L5's bracing was now based on an extended form of cross, known as X bracing; a radical departure from the twin parallel bracing favoured for the earlier 16" models.

Supporting a larger area in this way led to a relative lack of support beneath the bridge, at the very point where the downward tension was at its greatest. To compensate for this problem the arching was reduced around the bridge area to an almost flat profile. Indeed, some L5s from this period now evidence distinct sagging in this area of acute downward pressure.

Gibson's acoustical engineers were obviously well aware of this problem and their concern for the stability of the larger tops led to a degree of experimentation (circa 1937-39) where both methods of bracing were used concurrently. By 1939, however, parallel bracing had become the standard method for supporting the instrument's carved top.

The earlier advanced bodied L5s retained the same size "f" holes as the contemporaneous 16" version. Similarly the "f" holes were unbound until 1937 when enlarged "f" holes, commensurate with the increased size of the L5's larger body, were introduced.

Some L5s from 1937 were made with large unbound "f" holes but shortly afterwards these acquired a single-ply ivoroid binding. Additional black and white binding was also introduced for the body, fingerboard, peghead and pickguard. The position markers were reduced slightly in width, with extra markers added at frets 1 and 17. In keeping with the overall increase of black and white decoration, the bell shaped truss-rod cover was also given an eighth of an inch white border, which turned a nondescript access panel into an aesthetically striking adornment.

closeup of peghead and first fret inlay on 1930's L5

The reinstated point at the end of the fingerboard was also multibound, and acted as a graceful continuation of the fingerboard decorations. This significant increase in binding was carried over to the larger "F" holes, which were also bound, albeit more simply with a single strip of white celluloid.

1937 L5 (Note the large unbound "f" holes)

David Barbour with his late 30's L5

The earliest advanced bodied L5s retained the 24 3/4" scale fingerboard, but this was changed to 25 1/2" in 1937, to upgrade the model in line with the Super 400. The L5's hardware also underwent significant changes.

Hardware

The most noticeable change in the L5's hardware concerned the tailpiece. Up until this point two basic types had been used on the small-bodied models: a trapeze with welded crossbar, which the strings wrapped around, and a trapeze with a nut fastening crossbar, which the strings passed directly through. It was the second of these earlier designs which provided the basis for the new tailpiece. Strips of flat, pressed, brass replaced the thin metal rods previously used to support the crossbar. This provided a wider surface area which in turn provided more opportunity for decoration. By 1937/8 this tailpiece was changed further. The flat strips grew even larger and the open centrespace was covered by a silver art deco lozenge shape, mounted separately with two hidden nuts. Simple wavy patterns were engraved into the crossbar, as was the designation **L-5,** which had previously been the only decoration. The hinge at the bottom of the tailpiece, a unique feature of the earlier design, was eventually dropped, around 1937, predating the introduction of the "Varitone" tension adjuster (circa 1939).

This rigid tailpiece was the first to feature the new spring-loaded "Varitone" adjustment, accessible, by alum key, through a small hole.

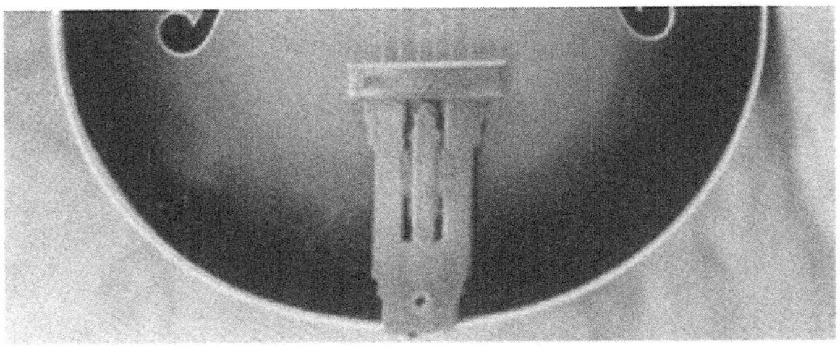

Closeup of Varitone tailpiece on early L5

The tension altering device itself was situated beneath the bottom plate–sandwiched, out of sight, between the carved spruce top and the underside of the tailpiece. By means of tightening or slackening the spring, the tailpiece could be raised or lowered, thereby altering the string tension and resulting playing action.

Whether Gibson's research and design team observed a good initial response for this innovation, or felt that it was intrinsically valuable as a useful sales pitch, is now unclear. They must have felt that it had lasting merit, for it was used for a further 36 years, not only on the various L5 models, but also on Super 400s and (albeit much later) Johnny Smiths.

Like the small bodied L5s which preceded them, the advanced models also underwent changes of machineheads. Early examples utilized the same open back, gold plated, Grovers found on the contemporaneous 16" model. But these were later changed to the larger Kluson, Sealfast, machines previously fitted as standard only on the Super 400. Kluson's Sealfast units were internally greased and sealed, making for a smoother operation, whilst at the same time preventing excessive wear on the gear cogs. As a result, the new tuners guaranteed a more accurate and reliable performance and were, not surprisingly, more popular.

The tulip shaped peg buttons of the Klusons were markedly different from the previous oval shaped Grovers and were plastic, as opposed to brass. Gold plated brass buttons were available however, as an optional extra, but were not fitted as a standard appointment until the mid '50s.

GUITAR DIGEST
by HY WHITE
STYLES
IMPROVISATIONS
AND
INTERPRETATIONS
FOR
SOLO GUITAR
AND
GUITAR WITH
ORCHESTRA
Including Solos featured with
WOODY HERMAN
On Records
EDWIN H. MORRIS & CO. LTD.
52 MADDOX STREET, LONDON, W.1
CHARLING MUSIC CORPN. NEW YORK
Authorised for sale in British Empire (except Canada) and Continent of Europe
E.M. 4527
3/6 net.

The Advanced Body L5 Players

The Roll Call of "advanced" body L5 players reads like a veritable Who's Who of the 1930's and 40's guitar playing fraternity. Country star Maybelle Carter progressed from a 16" L5 to an advanced body model, as did countless others. Well known L5 endorsees included, Carl Kress, Dick McDonough, George Smith, Joe Fava, Frank Worrell and Harry Volpe.

Carl Kress and Dick McDonough

Oscar Moore, Nat King Cole's "poll" winning guitarist was shown holding a 1930's advanced L5 on the cover of his 10" album: The Oscar Moore Quartet (Tampa 22). He later played a natural non-cutaway model from the 1940s, which had been factory equipped with a Charlie Christian pickup. An almost identical L5 was later used by his brother Johnny Moore in a popular trio called the Three Blazers.

Johnny Moore and the Three Blazers

Other high profile L5 players included Hy White, Tony Rizzi, Dave Barbour, Mundell Lowe, Tony Mottola, Van Moretti and Al Viola.

Mundell Lowe with early 1940s L5

Tony Mottola with the Tonight Show band

Al Viola

Van Moretti with 1940's L5

Sylvia Herald of the Hot Club of San Francisco

Elvis Presley with an early 1940's L5

Jackie Paris (left) at Sonny's Cafe in 1946

Ron Moore with late 30's L5

Marty Grosz with late 30's L5

Van Moretti with a 30's L5

CHAPTER 4

Cutaways And Cutbacks

THE L5P

A 1939 L5P serial # EA5571

The L5 Premier; "P" for short, made its debut in 1939. It was basically an advanced body L5 with a rounded cutaway. Gibson described the graceful lines of the soft cutaway as "Venetian", a term which has since been generically used to describe all of the company's rounded cutaways.

As with the innovative combination of violin "F" holes and arched tops, Gibson were once again ahead of the competition. Epiphone introduced their first cutaway archtops (Regent models) in 1949, as did D'Angelico and Stromberg. Gretsch were even later with their 1951 acoustic cutaway range.

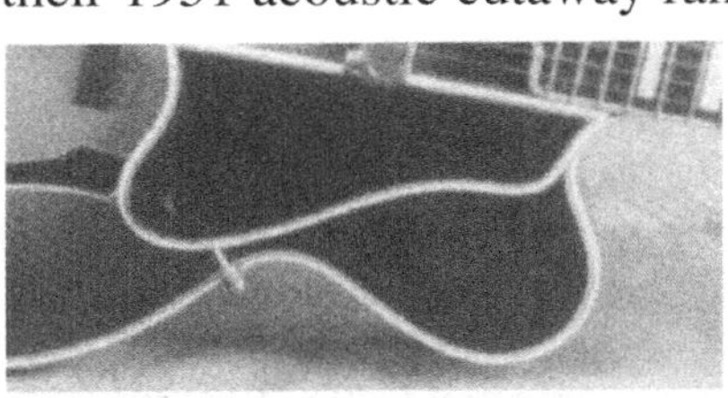

Photo: Close up of the Venetian cutaway on an L5P

It would be no exaggeration to suggest that Gibson changed the face of the steel string guitar, both electric and acoustic, with the launch of the L5 and Super 400 cutaway models. True, there were precedents. The Selmer Maccaferri, designed in the 1920s and marketed in the '30s, utilized an embryonic, if somewhat flat, cutaway. So too did the relatively obscure Shutt (circa 1910-20) and a few Prairie State models. But these were not true "F" hole archtops; neither were Gibson's 1920s STYLE "O"and the various Kay Kraft models of the 1930s.

Unlike the efforts of the aforementioned companies, the curves of Gibson's "Venetian" cutaway were symmetrically balanced with the instrument's overall profile. It looked perfectly natural –as if it **should** be there. Once again Gibson had instinctively "got it right." Furthermore the addition of an elegant cutaway was the logical fulfilment of the line, so much so that the L5P, later to be called the L5C ("c" for cutaway), was to eventually replace the non- cutaway model, output of which was gradually reduced until it was officially discontinued in 1958.

Besides spreading rapidly across the entire range of acoustic and electric archtops, the L5P's graceful rounded cutaway paved the way for such classic designs as the Gretsch 612O, the Gibson Les Paul and the Fender Telecaster. Gibson marketed its range of Premier cutaway guitars in a special supplementary brochure as shown :

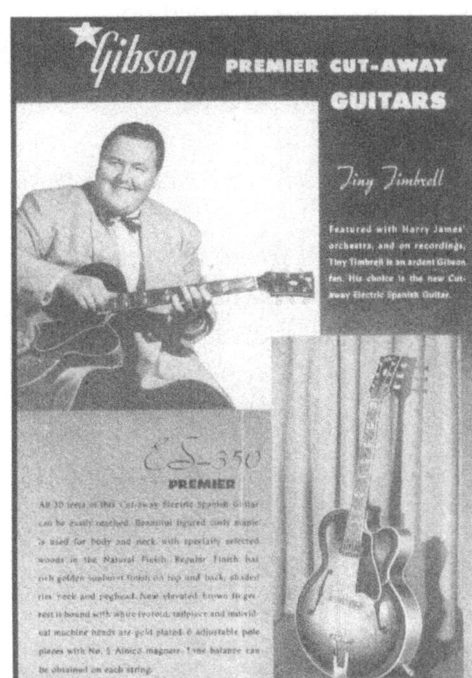

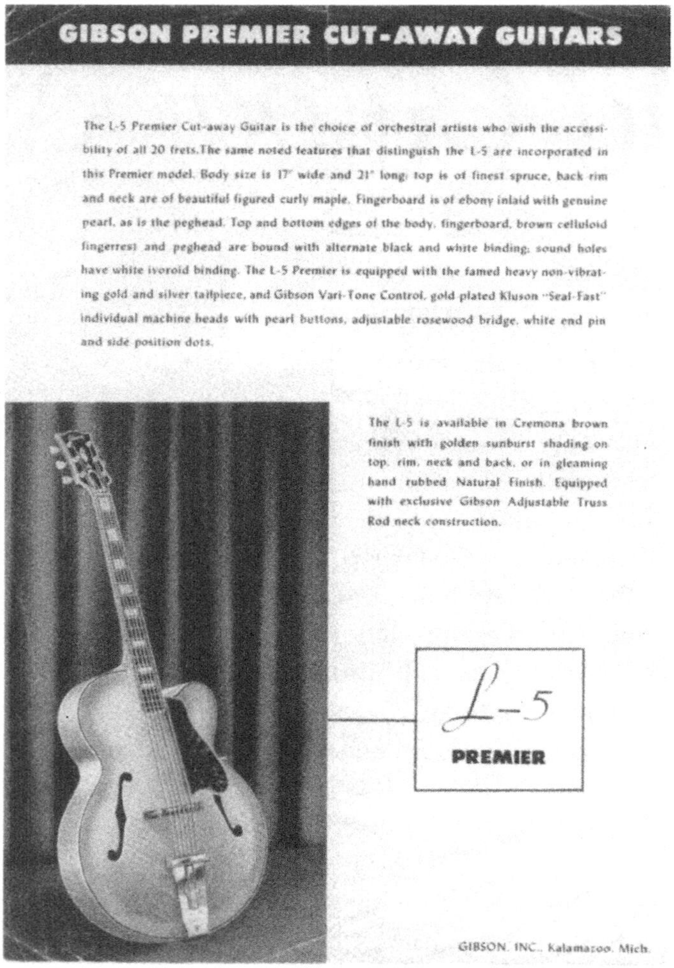

GIBSON PREMIER CUT-AWAY GUITARS

The L-5 Premier Cut-away Guitar is the choice of orchestral artists who wish the accessibility of all 20 frets. The same noted features that distinguish the L-5 are incorporated in this Premier model. Body size is 17" wide and 21" long; top is of finest spruce, back rim and neck are of beautiful figured curly maple. Fingerboard is of ebony inlaid with genuine pearl, as is the peghead. Top and bottom edges of the body, fingerboard, brown celluloid fingerrest and peghead are bound with alternate black and white binding; sound holes have white ivoroid binding. The L-5 Premier is equipped with the famed heavy non-vibrating gold and silver tailpiece, and Gibson Vari-Tone Control, gold plated Kluson "Seal-Fast" individual machine heads with pearl buttons, adjustable rosewood bridge, white end pin and side position dots.

The L-5 is available in Cremona brown finish with golden sunburst shading on top, rim, neck and back, or in gleaming hand rubbed Natural Finish. Equipped with exclusive Gibson Adjustable Truss Rod neck construction.

L-5
PREMIER

GIBSON, INC., Kalamazoo, Mich.

With the introduction of a cutaway came two important constructional changes in the L5's manufacture. Firstly, the earlier form of parallel bracing was reintroduced (for both cutaway and non–cutaway models) and secondly, the angle at which the neck joined the body was further reduced to accommodate the cutaway. This meant that the neck rake was positioned almost flush with the top, which allowed very little clearance for the fingerboard extension.

Owners of early L5Ps found that attaching a floating pickup, such as the newly designed DeArmond FHC GUITAR MIKE, was, usually, a very frustrating operation. The only way of doing so, on many of these early L5Ps, was to position the pickup midway between the end of the fingerboard and the bridge! By the early 1940s, however, the neck rake had been changed and the fingerboard extension was again able to float clear of the spruce top.

Other changes which accompanied the launch of the L5P, included the introduction of the Varitone tailpiece, described earlier, and, for an additional $10, the option of a natural finish. The extra premium for what was, in effect, a lack of colour, was introduced to compensate for the need to select unblemished timbers (knots, streaks and patches) and the extra time and care which had to be taken with glue joints and bindings. Untidy glue lines, it was found, could no longer be disguised with the dark edges of the sunburst stain.

1939 L5PN owned by Don DeMarco

The initial popularity of the natural finish can be seen from the instrument's increased shipping totals which for 1940, reveal that only 11 sunburst L5Ps were sold as compared to 40 natural ones.

Subtle changes were made during the cutaway L5's first decade (1939-1949). These included a more sloping angle for the "Gibson" headstock logo and the re-siting of the flowerpot inlay a fraction further away from the truss rod cover. Furthermore, the inlay itself was reduced from three separate pearl segments to two.

The plastic pegs of the Kluson Deluxe machine heads were also changed from large amber triangular buttons to smaller plastic ones which had a whiter pigment, designed expressly to simulate more expensive mother-of-pearl.

Following the war, in a period which lasted roughly between 1947 and 1949, many L5s were fitted with Brazilian rosewood fingerboards as a result of an immediate postwar shortage of ebony. Some also reverted to the pre 1937 24 3/4 inch scale.

During 1949 the signature, “script” style headstock logo was updated. the letters were more upright and consistant in width, balanced by downward tails on the G and N which hung below the other letters. The square character of each letter resulted in a logo which was less like a personal signature and more like a manufactured company emblem.

This bold modernistic print–face style was indicative of the company’s futuristic vision and rapidly increasing size.

1948 L5 P serial #A 1320

The War Effort

When, in 1941, America became involved in World War II, the manufacture of musical instruments was no longer considered to be of essential importance. Consequently, the company's output of guitars was drastically reduced and many "high end" instruments, such as the L5 and Super 400, were temporarily discontinued. Significant changes in specifications were also made to those models which remained in production, owing to an acute shortage of certain materials.

And, while some important developments took place in other areas, such as the introduction of the J45 and Southerner (S J), flat tops in 1942, the Research and Design team ceased work completely on important projects such as the construction and refinement of its electric archtops.

The handful of luthiers retained for the manufacture of guitars were also responsible for the company's warranty work, which provided a useful, yet low profile, contact with their market. The main body of Gibson's employees were, however, deployed on the war effort.

The principal manufacturing facility was redirected towards the provision of wartime supplies. Large outside contractors, such as Western Electric and R C A, were brought in to assemble the newly developed radar units. Components for submachine guns and a number of aircraft, were also mass produced in an operation which resulted in the acquisition of new machinery and tooling. The number of workers involved, in the various manufacturing processes at Kalamazoo, more than doubled in an attempt to keep pace with the demands of the various contractors.

These radical wartime activities were to have a profound effect upon the growth of Gibson following the cessation of hostilities. During the war, Gibson's accumulated woodworking expertise was such that they were awarded the highest accolades and awards from the War Department. More importantly, Gibson had not only inherited a larger workforce and the very latest machinery, it had also been at the forefront of technological development, pioneering engineering skills which the company was to further explore when, in 1947, the production of guitars was fully reinstated.

One such development was the use of high frequency radio waves which had been introduced to speed up the gluing of laminated glider skids. Gibson further refined this technique and carried it over to the construction of its guitars. So effective was its use that it is still employed today for gluing the tops, rims and center blocks of the ES range.

1940 L5P

C M I

On the 10th May 1944, CMI: (Chicago Musical Instruments) acquired a controlling interest in Gibson. Some internal politics followed when John Adams, who had been president of Gibson since 1902, resigned. Maurice Berlin, the founder of CMI became Gibson's Secretary and Treasurer, while Guy Hart held onto his position as General Manager, but at the same time assumed greater responsibility following Adams' resignation.

Berlin immediately instigated an increase in the size of Gibson's manufacturing plant, notably the provision of 15,000 square feet for the mill room and production area. He also authorised the purchase of new equipment and an improved lumber room facility. Furthermore, although the war had not yet ended, he turned his attention towards the company's reconstruction, by implementing the engineering and design work required to increase the range and improve the quality of guitars. When, in 1947, the manufacture of Gibson guitars was fully reinstated, Berlin's guidance and foresight was found to have anticipated the unprecedented post war demand for

Gibson guitars. His insistence upon establishing a nationwide network of authorized Gibson dealers, for example, had nurtured and improved public relations, which in turn resulted in a dramatic increase in sales. The following decade saw many innovative designs, as the company's range increased beyond recognition. One such development was the introduction of a full range of electric guitars, from the humble Les Paul Junior and ES125 to the electrified L5 and Super 400 (CES models).

L5P and L5C Players

Cutaway L5s were an immediate success; so much so that despite a brief hiatus in production, owing to wartime shortages, they were soon outselling the standard, non-cutaway, model.

One of the better known of the early users and endorsees was Allan Reuss . Reuss, and his L5PN, were regularly featured with popular dance bands including those led by Jimmy Dorsey, Benny Goodman and Jack Teagarden. He was also depicted with this new model in several of Gibson's 1940s catalogues.

During the late 30s Reuss made an attempt to cut back on the amount of time spent "on the road", by opening a teaching studio in New York. His reputation was such that the studio quickly became very successful, providing the profession with some of its leading guitarists for the next two decades. Housed in a small room, above the New York Band Instrument Company (a music store and repair shop), the studio provided a steady supply of customers for the Manhattan Gibson Guitar agency, which was coincidentally also based in the building. There can be little doubt that many of Reuss' budding students would have called in on Gibson agent Eddie Bell to purchase L5PNs similar to their teacher's.

Like Reuss, other prominent players of the period were also seen with L5Ps or Cs, in a succession of Gibson catalogues. These included Remo Palmier and Mundell Lowe, as well as less well known players like Stan Wilson and Danny Perri. Other sometime acoustic cutaway L5 players, included Arv Garrison, Muzzy Marcellino, Ike Isaacs, Tony Rizzi, Teddy Bunn and Marty Grosz .

Mundell Lowe playing an early L5 C

Tony Mottola

Danny Perri playing an early L5 CN

Stan Wilson

Remo Palmier with a sunburst L5 C

CHAPTER 5

Electrified Elegance

Early 1950s L5CESN

At the end of the war the American workforce returned to their avocations with a clearer and more purposeful, perspective. More importantly, they brought with them skills and expertise which endowed mass produced goods with a greater consistency of refinement. The economic expansion, which generally goes hand-in-hand with reconstruction, was unprecedented, and there was an enormous increase in demand for all manner of consumer goods. Amongst other so called "luxury items", the demand for musical instruments grew substantially following the war; a demand which necessitated many manufacturers to expand and retool. Many improvements in engineering, which had resulted from fuelling the war effort, were carried over into commercial manufacturing. Marketing and promotion were better co-ordinated and the rapport between producers and consumers was, in many instances, enhanced.

While these "improved" conditions applied to many of the corporate industries during the honeymoon period which followed the war, some far-sighted managers also began working much closer with their research and design departments in order to ensure that their companies would be one step ahead of the competition.

The general "shake up" caused by changes in the management and ownership of Gibson in 1944, provided an ideal opportunity for consolidation, growth and innovation. Consolidation and growth were evident from the outset, with significant increases in the square footage of accommodation and number of employees. Innovation followed, coming to the forefront in 1948 with the appointment of Ted McCarty, who, along with electronics engineers Seth Lover and Walter Fuller, went on to pioneer crutial designs and components in the development of the electric guitar.

In 1948, Gibson's range of electric guitars consisted of the ES125, the ES150, the ES300 and its cutaway counterpart: the ES350P. No less than 25 electric guitars were introduced during the ensuing decade under the direction of Ted McCarty and John Huis. The launch of the L5CES, alongside the Super 400CES, at the 1951 New York Trade Show marked the depth of Gibson's commitment to the electric guitar.

The launch of the L5CES and its larger stablemate, the SUPER 400CES, can be seen as the logical culmination of Gibson's electro acoustic line. Budget models, such as the ES100 had been around since the 1930s, enabling the non-professional, the sceptical and the student player to sample the delights of the newly developed electric guitar.

As the guitar superseded the banjo, in the growing number of dance bands, a new breed of guitar player emerged whose criteria for a good instrument consisted of volume, penetration and cutting power. Aesthetics and workmanship were secondary. In an attempt to satisfy these changing demands, instruments grew increasingly larger. Sixteen inch body guitars were advanced to seventeen, and companies like Gibson, Epiphone and Gretsch introduced new models with inflated dimensions and equally larger than life names.

During the 1940s the DeArmond microphone company introduced an ingenious device (The FCH Guitar microphone) which attached to an archtop guitar, with little fuss, and could be easily taken off again when it wasn't needed. While this enabled literally thousands of guitar players to sample the joys of amplification literally overnight, it was still not an entirely perfect solution.

In the meantime Gibson were displaying a marked commitment to the electric guitar, as evidenced by the expansion of their range to include the ES125, ES130, ES150, ES250, ES300, ES350, ES5, ES175 and ES140. The latter three were introduced under the direction of Maurice Berlin, Ted McCarty and John Huis, who, having prophetically anticipated consumer demand, had resolved to increase and broaden the electric guitar range.

Ted McCarty was, like Orville Gibson and Lloyd Loar before him, a man of great vision and inventiveness. The designs and developments which came together under his cataclysmic leadership, either by direct engineering input, or by support and guidance, marked the most successful and prolific period thus far in Gibson's development of the electric guitar.

The L5CES was introduced in late 1951, a month before the unveiling of the Super 400CES. Thirty one sunburst and eight natural models were shipped during the remaining months of 1951.

The first L5CES models were fitted with two single coil P90 pickups and the wiring circuitry of earlier single pickup models such as the ES150, ES250, ES300 and ES175 was doubled up to maximise tonal variation. Consequently each pickup had its own tone and volume control which meant that both pickups could be isolated or combined as required,via a three way toggle switch mounted on the lower treble bout.

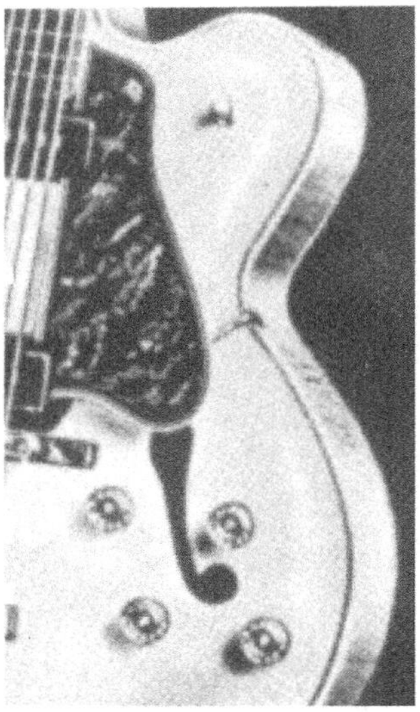

Toggle switch and controls configuration.

So effective was this, four controls and a selector switch, configuration that it was immediately carried over onto the Super 400CES, the ES295, the ES350, the Les Paul and the ES175; indeed it would soon become the standard circuitry for the great majority of Gibson's twin pickup guitars.

Van Hoose suggested that the L5CES "was designed to incorporate a combination of features from the L5C and the ES5, Gibson's premier electric guitar from 1948 through 1950" (1991 p113).*

The L5CES was certainly based upon the L5C, and retained much the same dimensions, woods and ornamentation. However, while it is true that the top was carved a little thicker and the parallel braces widened to accommodate the routing for the P90s, there is little further evidence that the ES5 provided any kind of model for the L5CES. Furthermore, the ES5 has three pickups, plywood construction and markedly different electric circuitry.

Early catalogues clearly show that the ES5 was itself based upon the L5C, but given laminated woods for optimum performance as a purely "electric" instrument.

* ***"Gibson Super 400- Art of the Fine Guitar"***

L5CN

ES5N

CES Version I (1951-54)

The author playing a 1951 L5CES at the Arlington, TX Guitar Show

The first CES L5 was ostensively an "electrified" L5C. It utilized the same basic ornamentation, timbers and hardware, excepting, of course, its newly acquired electrical components. However, whilst the cosmetic specifications were identical to the L5C, there were fundamental differences in construction between the two models. In order to support the additional weight of the pickup's toggle-switch, controls and wiring harness, the L5CES' internal bracing system was modified in three ways. Firstly the parallel braces were given additional bulk, to support the top more effectively and secondly they were set further apart from one another, to allow room for routing the pickup cavities. Additionally the remaining struts were carved a little heavier to give the top an increased overall stiffness.

The single coil P90 pickups, developed by Walter Fuller, were already in use on Gibson's other electro-acoustic guitars such as the ES5, the ES350 and the ES175. Each P90 pickup sat beneath a 1 $^{1}/_{2}$" wide black plastic cover (Royalite) which was screwed to the L5's spruce top through two flat, triangular, side wings commonly referred to nowadays as "dog ears". By 1952 the plastic pickup covers were marginally wider (1 $^{5}/_{8}$") and flatter. They were also molded from a different grade of plastic which had less of a glossy appearance.

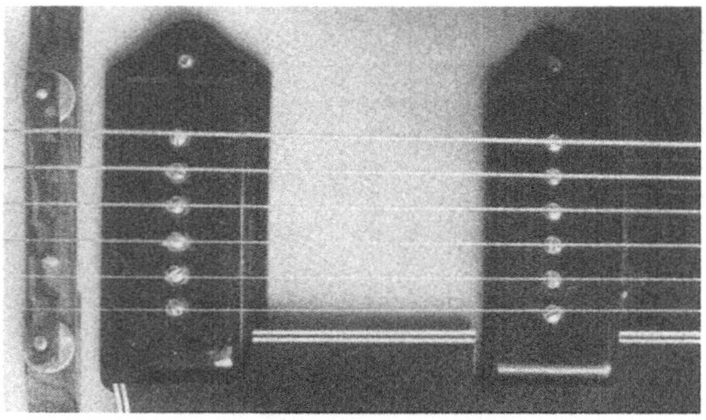

Close up of P90s showing "dog ear"

Both neck and bridge pickups had height adjustable screw threaded magnetic pole pieces. The bridge pickup utilized a flat, plastic, riser block which sat beneath the pickup flange. This gave the bridge pickup the additional height needed to place the pole pieces closer to the strings. The increased space between the bridge pickup and the strings was due to the rake of the neck and its concomitant distance between the strings and the top.

While the other electric components were common to contemporaneous ES models, the three-way toggle switch and independent pickup circuits were new. As early as 1954, the same circuitry was fitted as standard to all of Gibson's twin pickup guitars. The same bound tortoise-shell pickguard, plastic buttoned gold plated Kluson tuners and rosewood pre-cut compensating bridge used on the concurrent L5C, completed the CES' appointments.

The first L5CES' were available in a dark sunburst or natural finish, but as with their acoustic counterparts, natural instruments were more costly and produced in significantly lower numbers. (See Appendix C Shipping Totals).

Sal Salvador with P90 L5CES

C E S Version 2 (1954-57)

The construction, timbers and ornamentation of the second variant L5CES were similar to those found on the first model. By 1956 a wider strip of white celluloid binding had replaced the thin wooden insert on the inside upper rim of the cutaway. This extra width of plastic compensated for the curvature of the arched top.

There were also, three significant changes of hardware, the most obvious being the upgrading of pickups from P90s to Alnico No 5's. Utilizing a similar basic single coil design, Seth Lover perfected a new pickup during the latter part of 1952 and the early part of 1953. This "upgraded" unit had the same 10,000 turns of wire as the P90, but in place of the usual six screw-threaded pole pieces, individual Alnico magnets were used.

These individual magnets were spring mounted and therefore height adjustable, via a small adjacent screw; mounted in the plastic cover (in twos) between the exposed tips of the individual magnets.

Fitted firstly to the Super 400CES, and then the L5CES, Les Paul Custom and Byrdland respectively, Gibson's 1953 catalogue announced that the extra large individually adjustable Alnico No5 magnets gave "greater sustaining power". While this may have been the case, they were also susceptible to the same inherent hum problems as their predecessors and were eventually discontinued in favour of a more efficient hum cancelling pickup.

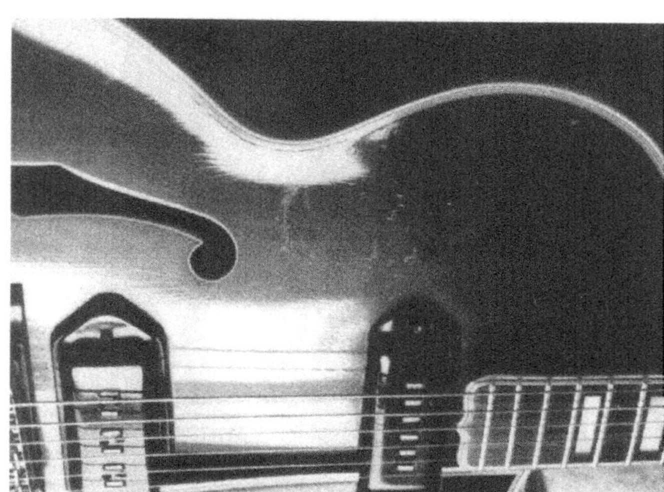

Closeup of alnico pickups on second version L5CES

The second change of hardware took place during early 1955, when the rosewood bridge, with a base which fitted entirely flush with the contour of the carved top, was modified along violin principles.

The new bridge base now had two separate and distinct feet, which made contact with the top in a similar manner to those bridges used for violins, violas, 'cellos and double basses.

Reduced mass in the centre of the new bridge provided enough flexibility for it to be fitted without recourse to the time consuming labour of contouring and matching its surface to the curvature of the top. This provided many benefits, for not only did it save time and cost in manufacture, it also meant that the new bridges were compatible with all of the company's archtop guitars and that bridge replacement was no longer a major undertaking.

The original "single foot" rosewood bridge continued to be fitted as stock, however, on the L5C, as its extra bulk and greater contact with the top was considered important for the transmission of acoustic tone and volume. Conversely, the new double footed bridge was given a metal top which significantly inhibited acoustic tone, but compensated for this fact by offering far greater accuracy of intonation.

Filed for patent in 1952, but not finally approved until 1956, Gibson, nevertheless, began marketing this aptly named "tune-o-matic" bridge in 1953. It was fitted exclusively on electric models, such as Les Paul Customs and ES5s as well as top of the line acoustics like the L5CES and Super 400's. The bridge itself consisted of a metal housing with six, screw adjustable, saddles placed longitudinally of the strings and transversly of the bridge. These could be easily moved via a simple screw either forwards, to shorten the string length and thus sharpen the pitch, or backwards, to lengthen the string and thus flatten the pitch. This ingenious mechanism was apparently the brainwave of Ted McCarty who filed the patent on Gibson's behalf.

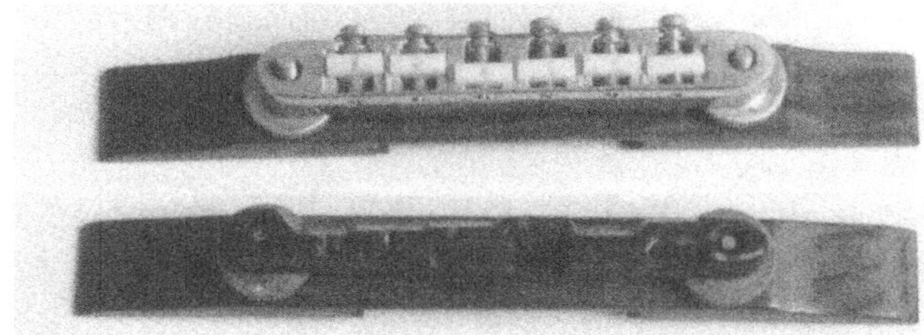

Rosewood and tune–omatic bridges

Alnico L5CES with tune-o-matic bridge

The third change of hardware concerned the plastic tuning buttons of the L5's Kluson DeLuxe Machineheads, which were replaced by gold plated metal buttons of a similar size and shape in late 1956. These were initially used on the first batch of Byrdlands in 1955 and gradually migrated across to the other " top of the line" guitars such as the J200, Les Paul Custom, and Super 400 and L5C and CES. Unlike the tune-o-matic bridge, which was only fitted to the CES, the new tuners were also fitted to the L5C. By mid 1955 the gold 'barrel' tone and volume control knobs were also replaced by the somewhat smaller 'bonnet' knobs, which were subsequently used until 1960.

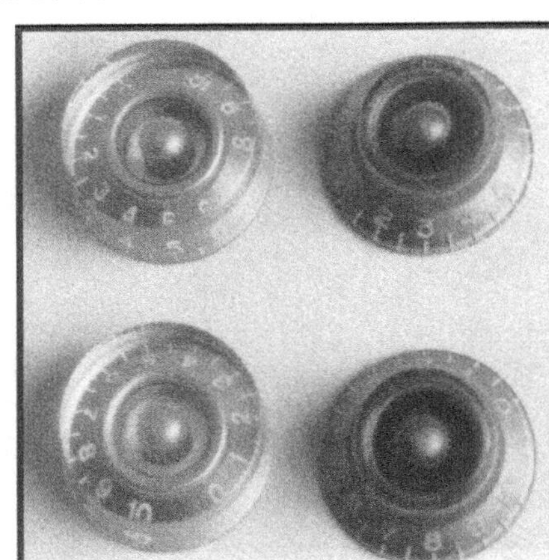

Barrel knobs and the bonnet knobs which replaced them

Shipping Totals for the L5CES 1951 - 1957

	1951	1952	1953	1954	1955	1956	1957
L5CES	31	29	25	30	19	23	22
L5CESN	8	17	18	20	31	32	15

1956-1957

With the exception of their cheaper models, such as the ES120, 125, 135, 140 and 225, Gibson modernised the bulk of its electric line in 1957. Indeed, the period between 1955 and 1957 was a 'golden age' in the growth and development of Gibson's electric guitar range, which saw both the arrival of radical new designs (the ES5, 350T, Byrdland and Flying V prototype) and the introduction of the double-coil humbucking pickup.

In the ensuing five years (1958-1963), the company produced a range of electric guitars which are considered by players and collectors alike, to be amongst their finest

The P90 L5CES Players

Scotty Moore with his P90 L5CES

Scotty Moore is probably the best known "P90" L5CES player. Despite the fact that he only used the L5CES for a brief period, it was featured in the 1957 film LOVING YOU and on several important contemporaneous Presley recordings.

Retrospectively, however, Moore's natural finish L5CES proved little more than a stepping stone between his trusty ES295 and the Alnico Super 400CESN he used for the following decade.

Excepting the occasional non jazz player like Scotty Moore, Tony Mottola and Joe Sgro, the L5CES was mostly used by jazz guitarists. Mundell Lowe (1922–), Dave Barbour (1912-1965), Allen Hanlon (1919-1986), Bill Leavitt (1925-1990) and George Barnes (1921-1977) were all one-time users of P90 L5CES's.

Allen Hanlon

George Barnes

The Alnico L5CES Players

Wes Montgomery with a L5CES and alnico pickups

While the Alnico 5 pickup suffered from the same electrical interference as the P90, namely an audible background hum from neon-lights, electric motors and other kinds of electrical equipment, it nevertheless produced a noticeably clearer sound with greater separation between the treble and bass strings.

This improved audio fidelity was particularly well received by jazz guitarists, who were able to enjoy higher distortion-free thresholds. The pickup's improved clarity and separation was particularly well utilized by Wes Montgomery (1925-1968), whose ground breaking octave style was ideally suited to the Alnico unit.

As Montgomery's influence spread, so too did the talk about his unusual playing style, as well as his choice of instrument. Other jazz guitarists playing on the West Coast whilst Wes was guesting at clubs like the Hungry I and Tsubos included Dempsey Wright (1929–) with Harry Babasin's Jazz Pickers, and Ray Crawford (1924–) with the Curtis Amy Sextet, both of whom played sunburst Alnico L5s similar to Wes'.

Kenny Burrell also played an Alnico L5, with a natural finish, during the late 1950s, in an albeit short period of transition between his ES175DN and various D'Angelicos. Don Arnone used the model during his role as rhythm guitarist on important recordings by Mundell Lowe and Tal Farlow, while sessioners Tony Mottola (1918–) and Tommy Tedesco (1930–) also utilized the new model to meet the challenging demands of their studio work.

Perry Lopez a fine player who divided his time between sessions, teaching and jazz gigs, was depicted in the company's 1960 and 61 catalogues with an unusual, single pickup, Alnico L5CESN; a model which was never officially offered as part of the CES range.

Perry Lopez with single pickup alnico L5

Dempsey Wright

Wes Montgomery

"... whatever he does comes alive, the mark of a true artist"

A self-taught master of the jazz guitar, until recently Wes had done all of his playing (except for two years with Lionel Hampton) in and around his native Indianapolis. He didn't cut his first record album until late in 1959.

But the Montgomery sound had long been known and respected among professional musicians. And, once "discovered," the news of this man from Indiana spread to jazz enthusiasts everywhere.

What is the Montgomery sound? It's an exciting quality that makes Montgomery music come alive. It's a terrific swing, the ability to build solos dramatically, to climax after climax. A sense of tightness. A smooth, easy, flowing style. It's the sound of great jazz . . . from a guitar.

Most of all . . . the Montgomery sound is a soft, delicate, exceedingly sensitive kind of music that is created deep within his being. Yes, Wes Montgomery plays a truly incredible jazz guitar. And his guitar is a **Gibson**

Gibson, Inc.
Kalamazoo, Michigan

CHAPTER 6

PAF Models

The introduction and installation of a new kind of pickup, in 1957, marked the birth of the modern L5CES. Indeed, subsequent variants were based on this classic model to such an extent that the early PAF version was to become the very personification of an electric L5.

By 1962 another permanent change was made affecting the construction of the neck. These changes in components and construction proved long term, the legacy of which can still be seen on current models. Other design features such as the new style of cutaway, introduced in 1960, and the unprecedented use of plywood backs, for CES models, proved unpopular and were thus relatively short-lived.

The P A F Humbucking pickup

Gibson's new humbucking pickup (PAF)

During the autumn of 1957, Gibson made a significant departure from its single-coil P90 and Alnico pickups in favour of an innovatory hum cancelling pickup, appropriately called the 'humbucker'. From this period onwards, the P90 was relegated to models beneath the ES175 in the electric range and the Alnico unit was discontinued (excepting the various Les Paul Custom reissues).

The humbucker was expressly designed to be a quieter pickup than its predecessors. Furthermore, its assembly configuration utilised a similar, spring-loaded, tilting mechanism to the earlier bar pickup, but in a more compact form. This, coupled with adjustable pole pieces (the only adjustment available on previous pickups), made the humbucker Gibson's most versatile pickup thus far, a pickup which could be adjusted to accommodate a variety of playing techniques, whilst operating quietly at increasingly high volumes.

Its suspended assembly also enabled the humbucker to hang freely inside the body of the guitar, floating free from the top rather than being screwed directly to it. This reduced the potential for feedback and thus made it possible to play electro acoustic guitars, like the L5CES fitted with humbuckers, at considerably higher volumes than similar guitars fitted with P90s or Alnicos. It also allowed for greater flexibility in determining the angle of rake at which the neck joined the body.

Since the days of Gibson's first single-coil pickup, the so-called "Charlie Christian", electric guitar players had been complaining about the conspicuous hum and buzz caused by electro-magnetic interference. This interference, which was also common to the subsequent P90 and Alnico pickups, emanated from transformers, fluorescent lights or electric motors which were situated within close proximity to the guitar.

As the position and use of these electric appliances were, in many cases, beyond the player's direct control, the interference often proved detrimental to the performance and it was clear that a viable alternative had to be found.

If Gibson was to maintain its pre-eminent position in the electric guitar market, a more practical "quieter" pickup had to be introduced, and introduced quickly. Because single coil pickups were extremely susceptible to interference, electronics engineer, Seth

Lover, hit upon the idea of creating a unit based upon the humbucking field coil principle, originally used for energised loudspeakers. Whilst this method had long been discarded in the manufacture of loudspeakers, Lover took the same principle and hooked up two coils, wired in series, but out of phase with each other. This allowed the interference received by one coil to be phase cancelled by the other, thereby eliminating the unwanted hum.

Whilst Gibson officially introduced the humbucking pickup in 1957, trials to develop a quieter unit had begun as early as 1953. Seth Lover and Walter Fuller were the principal engineers ultimately responsible for the new unit but it was Lover who eventually registered the "humbucking" design with the US Patent Office on 22nd June, 1955. Owing to several similar pickup designs, which had also been registered, Gibson's humbucker patent was still under negotiation in 1957, the year in which the company first began to use it for the ES175.

Apart from the initial batch of humbuckers, the new pickup had a tiny black and silver label glued to its underside. This carried the words "Patent Applied For", which provided the origin of the now legendary PAF abbreviation.

The decal, it was hoped, would discourage would-be competitors from copying the design, little did Gibson know the fun and mystique that this tiny label would eventually generate.

Even though the patent was granted on 28th June 1959 (Patent No. 2896491), 'Patent Applied For' labels continued to be used until the beginning of 1963, when a new decal showing a confusingly different patent number took its place. It seems, however, that for a period of time, both labels were used on an ad hoc basis. It is not unusual, therefore, to find L5CESs from 1963 and 1964 with a combination of PAF and patent number pickups.

The much sought after PAF pickup

Florentine Cutaways

With the third type of pickup came several other significant changes, the most radical of which took place during the course of 1960. The biggest single change involved reworking the profile of the Venetian cutaway. Accredited at various times both to Ted McCarty and Kenny Burrell, the new "Florentine" cutaway had the same sharp pointed, scooped-out, design as the cutaway found on the ES175. This deeper cutaway provided easy access to the higher frets, but necessitated a longer internal neck block to accommodate the additional depth. Similarly the L5's tortoiseshell pickguard had to be shortened and was subsequently redesigned so as to screw into the top of the instrument instead of being pinned to the side of the neck as was previously the case (and continued to be the case on the Venetian cutaway L5C).

Between 1962 and 1969, the great majority of L5CESs utilized the Florentine cutaway design, whilst the concurrent L5C retained the earlier rounded, Venetian, cutaway style. A handful of Florentine cutaway, acoustic, L5s are known to exist but these were made as custom orders and are, therefore, extremely rare.

L5CESN as shown in Gibson's early 1960's catalog, despite the fact that the venetian cutaway had been discontinued

The Rubber Grommet

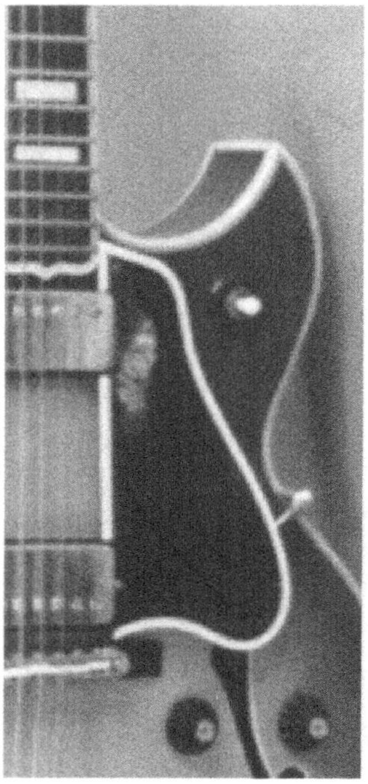

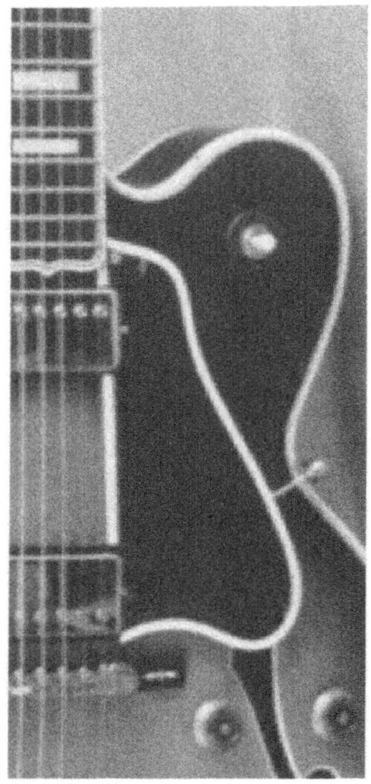

Shortly after Gibson changed pickups from Alnico to PAFs, other subtle, design features and changes of components were introduced.

After the initial run of PAF L5CESs, a black rubber grommet was added to the mounting of the three-way pickup selector switch. As well as improving the instrument's aesthetic appearance, the rubber grommet served two important practical functions: firstly, it cushioned the switch against potential damage; and secondly, it muted the clicking which could be heard whenever the switch was used.

Because it had previously been mounted directly into the wood, the vibrations caused by activating the selector switch were amplified by the pickups and unintentionally transmitted to the amplifier resulting in an unwanted *click.* The introduction of a rubber grommet, which was really a kind of double washer, provided a simple, yet effective, solution to this problem.

In fact, so successful was this grommet that it soon found its way onto all of Gibson's premium quality electro-acoustics from the ES175 to the Super 400CES.

Other Changes

Other structural changes included the introduction of a three-piece laminated maple neck (with mahogany seams), which superseded the traditional two-piece version in 1962, and the introduction of a one-piece laminated back (CES models only).

During the early 60s Gibson appear to have been inconsistent in their construction of CES models. Two-piece plywood and two piece solid maple backs can be randomly found on guitars from this period. Generally speaking, however, the solid backs were restricted to L5Cs, L5CTs and the handful of CESs with venetian cutaways.

In 1960, cosmetic gold caps were added to the bonnet knobs, carrying the words "TONE" or "VOLUME" in upper case letters. Serial numbers, previously to be found only on the orange label under the bass 'f' hole, were now also impressed on to the upper end of the back of the headstock.

Julius Bellson's 'A' numbering system established as far back as April 1947, was discontinued in February 1961, when a five digit numbers only scheme was introduced and used on both label and headstock. By 1963, the numbers had risen to six digits, after which time, co-incidentally, the company's stock of decalled PAFs began to dwindle.

1955 L5 CES

1942 L5N

1952 L5C

1975 L-5 CES

George Goebel L5CT

1960 Florentine cutaway L5CES

A transitional L5CES and close up of the Varitone tailpiece

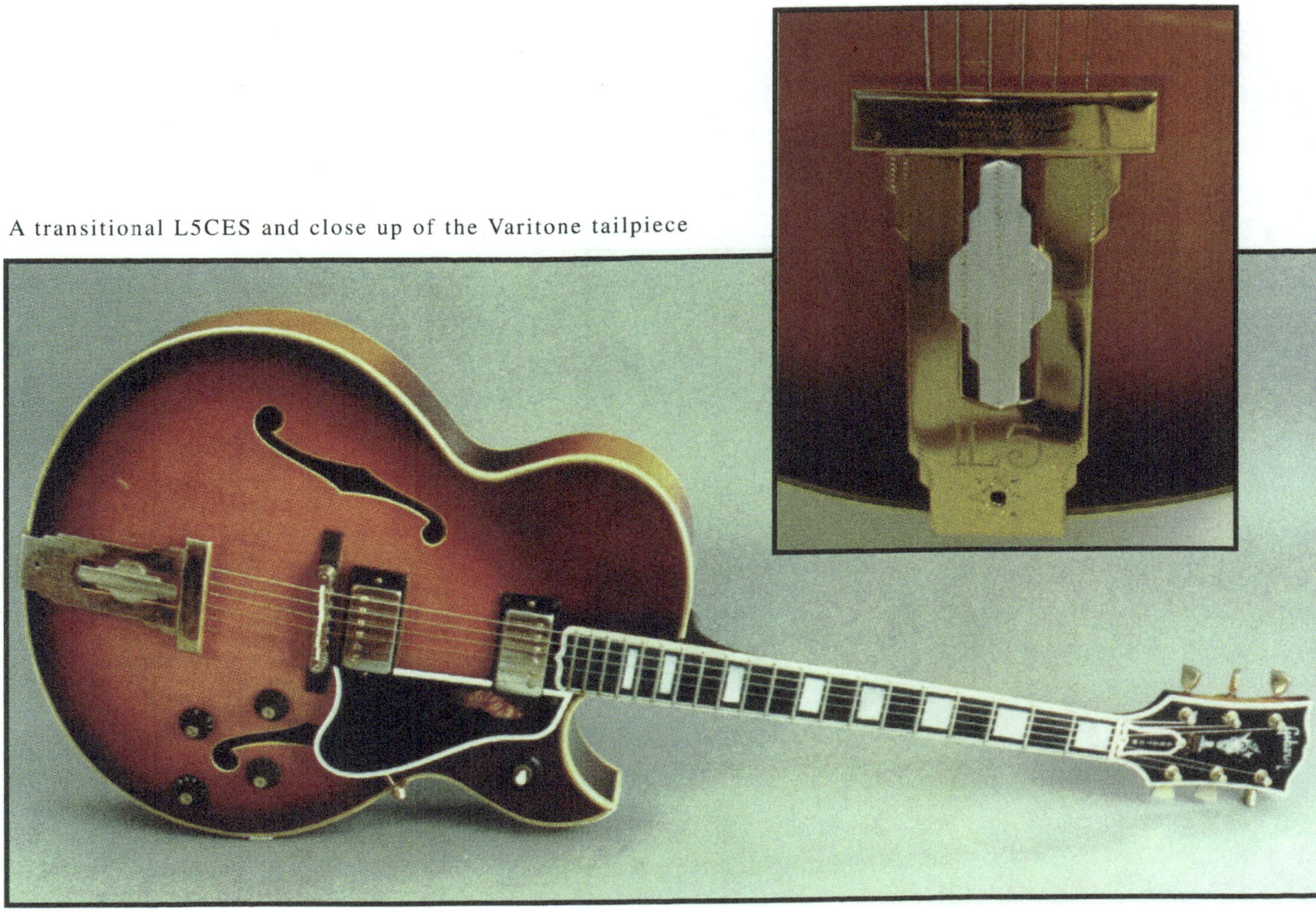

Photo by Rusty Russel

Scotty Moore with late 1980's L5, in his home studio outside Nahville

L5CES 50th Anniversary, 1986 Gruhn Guitars Inc.

A beautiful example of an early cutaway L5

Photo: Walter Carter, courtesy Gibson Guitar Corp.

L-5CESN, 1994 Current production model in the Historic Collection

Photo: Walter Carter, courtesy Gibson Guitar Corp.

'34 L-5 Reissue custom made for the Sara Lee Classic, 1996. Presented to Meg Mallon, the winner of the Sara Lee Classic women's golf tournament. The '34 L-5 is a production model from the Historic Collection, based on the 16-inch acoustic L-5

"Surf Guitar" Out take from the Grant Geissman CD photo session, by Loni Specter © 1997

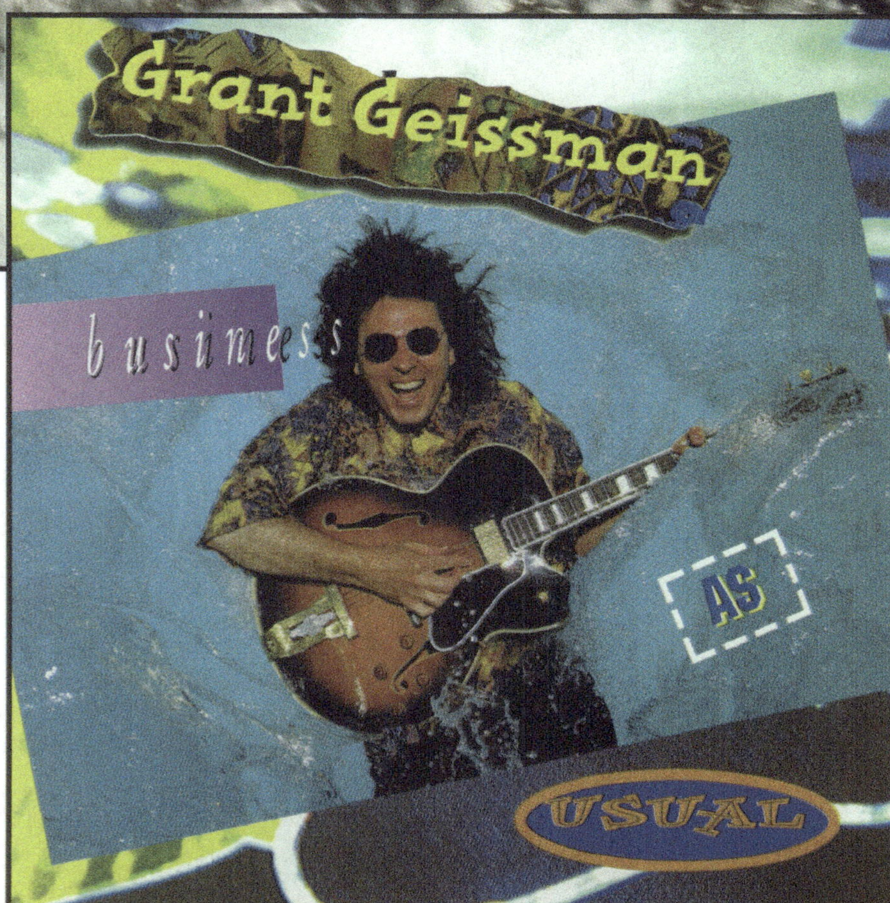

For the cover of Grant Geissman's 1995 *Business As Usual* album Mike McGuire of the Gibson Custom Shop arranged for an L5 to be loaned for submersion and other cruel and unusual punishment. The result was this spectacular shot, achieved on the third take with a rapid shutter camera by Loni Specter. Sadly, the guitar itself didn't fare as well, proving that L5's and water don't mix. After the photo's were taken the guitar was sent back to Gibson and put to rest.

A 1940's L5N with Varitone tailpiece

Photo's courtesy Jim Hahn.

George Gobel L-5CT #90633383, 1993

This guitar is rare in that it is about 1/8" too thick, you can see the difference in thickness from the side profile photo's on this page and p.59

Photo's courtesy Jim Hahn.

George Gobel L-5CT #92693847 made in 1993 for Jim Hahn after he bought the red one on page 58.
Both guitars have BJB pickups, 24 3/4 scale lengths and are X braced.

A 1950's L5C with missing pickguard and non-original ebony bridge

A late 1980s L5CES, notice the wooden appliqué, carrying the L5 designation in the tailpiece

Late 1980's L5CES

Wes Montgomery L5, with removed pickguard

One of Wes Montgomery's custom built single pickup L5s prior to restoration

The L5CT and L5CES Thin

1961 and 1963 L5CESTs

Although the Byrdland and the ES350 had already paved the way for a thinline L5, it took the, then popular comedian and entertainer, George Gobel to get the ball rolling. Andy Nelson, a one time clinitian for Gibson, who readers may have seen depicted in 1950s and 60s Gibson advertisements and catalogues, remember one particular meeting with Gobel in early 1958. Following his performance in a show at the Palmer House Chicago, George Gobel caught up with Nelson for a social get together and relaxing after-hours drink.

Having used a Super 400 as part of his act for many years Gobel, wanted to know if Gibson made anything of a similar quality, but with smaller dimensions. This was born out of necessity as Gobel was a rather stocky, yet small man, who appeared to be literally engulfed by the Super 400s massive bout. Nelson recalled:

I had been mulling over the idea of having Gibson do a special guitar for George. It was to be a thinner, shorter scale model with a thin X braced top, instead of the parallel top bracing preferred by Gibson President Ted McCarty and Vice-President Julius Bellson, among others .... The thinner body and shorter scale would make it more comfortable for George to hold and play. After talking to George about it, we also decided that the body should be bright cherry red to make it show up better on stage and on television, newly in colour in some areas. (Nelson, A. 1992, 20th Century Guitar)

Hank Garland and Billy "Byrd" had, of course, modelled the "Byrdland" guitar on the concept of a thin bodied L5CES. Indeed, a batch of four experimental L5CES had been made (2 natural and 2 sunburst) in April 1955. Two (serial numbers A20469 and A20470) were given to Billy Byrd and Hank Garland respectively and the original Byrdland advert shows both players with these L5CES prototypes before the introduction of the Byrdland tail piece and tune–o–matic bridge. The George Gobel model was, as can be seen from Nelson's description, different in several respects.

Hank Garland with the second L5CES/Byrdland prototype

The L5CT programme was approved by Gibson's Sales Manager, Clarence Havenga, towards the close of 1958. Gobel's guitar (Serial Number A27318) was in fact shipped on the 20th March 1958.

George Gobel's 1958 L5CT

L-5CN

The L-5 has held its enviable position as an exceedingly popular orchestra guitar for many years . . . a wonderfully rich tone, easy playing action, and beautiful cutaway styling are among the reasons.

Features: Carved top of finest close-grained spruce, carved back of highly figured curly maple with matching rims, and white-black-white ivoroid binding. Slim, fast, low-action, three-piece curly maple neck with adjustable truss rod. Ebony fingerboard with black pearl inlays. Rosewood adjustable bridge. Hand bound pickguard. Exclusive adjustable tailpiece. Gold-plated metal parts and Sealfast individual machine heads with metal buttons.

17" wide, 21" long, 3⅜" deep . . .
25½" scale, 20 frets

L-5CN Natural finish
L-5C Sunburst finish
600 Faultless plush-lined case
606 Faultless, flannel-lined case
ZC-6 Deluxe zipper case cover

L-5CN

L-5 CT Thin Body Cutaway

Developed expressly for George Gobel with the same fine features as L-5CN . . . plus thinner body in gleaming cherry-red finish.

17" wide, 21" long, 2⅜" thin . . .
24¾" scale, 20 frets

L-5CT Cherry finish
603 Faultless plush-lined case
ZC-6 Deluxe zipper case cover

The 1958 example, which utilized the regular 25 ½" L5 scale length, was a "one-off" built expressly for Gobel, as the pre-production prototype was not in fact completed until 1959. Similarly 1959 saw the models' commercial release and Gibson's ledgers show that 23 were shipped during its initial year. Built more or less to Nelson's specifications, with the exception of the X bracing, the L5CT was never officially designated as the George Gobel model, although it is now commonly referred to as such.

The L5CT was listed separately in Gibson's 1960 catalogue, although it was not depicted. By 1962, details of the L5CT were included in and amongst the general columns about acoustic L5s but, excepting occasional custom orders, production of the L5CT had already ceased.

Gibson never "officially" offered an electric version of the thin-bodied L5, although several do exist. These were either equipped with the same dual PAF electrics as the regular L5CES, or with a Charlie Christian pickup.

One of the most famous examples belonged to Hank Garland (serial number A30620) and is depicted on the cover of his classic recording JAZZ WINDS FROM A NEW DIRECTION:

A rare L5CT Crest

Early 60's L5CT with its original hardshell case

The CES versions were finished in sunburst or natural, and fitted with the standard 25 1/2" scale length fingerboard. Only a handful were made and the model was consequently never catalogued. Neither was the L5CT-CREST, an ornately decorated thin-bodied version of the Florentine cutaway L5CT. Andy Nelson continues the story:

"The original "Crest", built to my specifications, was a highly decorated L5CT. I had the factory build six of them. I personally sold every one of them at the unheard of price (in those days) of $1500!

Construction details included the use of the new for 1960 (on L5s) Florentine cutaway. The body was painted in Bright cherry red. The 22 fret neck used Super 400 style split block inlays, and had a knight's head peghead inlay (simulating a Gibson family "crest" thus the name). The tuners were extra fancy gold plated Grover Imperials. The tailpiece was a gold-plated custom unit, and the two humbuckers used Gibson's "variatone" (stereo) wiring. (ibid.)

The PAF L5CES Players

Of all the electric L5s, the PAF version has proved the most popular and enduring. Like the ES175 and Super 400CES of the same period, the PAF L5CES has become a jazz guitar "icon" helped, in no small part, by the pervasive influence of Wes Montgomery.

It would be no exaggeration to suggest that Montgomery put the L5CES on the map. Whilst others had used the instrument to good effect in the past, Montgomery raised its profile significantly, not only through his many magnificent live performances, but also through pictures on album sleeves, magazine articles and related promotional material. The covers of BOSS GUITAR (Riverside RLP 459) and FULL HOUSE (Riverside RLP 12-434) for example, show Wes with a late '50s L5CESN, while the cover of MOVIN WES (VERVE VLP 9092) and the liner notes of FULL HOUSE show him with an early florentine model.

These recordings have proved enormously influential and continue to sell, in healthy numbers, following their reformat onto compact disc. If "would be" jazz guitarists were inspired by Wes' playing, it was only natural that they should aspire to obtain a similar instrument; thus for many the PAF L5CES became the Holy Grail of jazz guitars. Indeed, there was nothing unusual in this, guitars have always sold because of their association with top players; remember that Eddie Lang, for example, had sent an entire generation of banjo players hunting for 16″ Gibson L5s during the late 20s.

One of the young players to take note of Montgomery's choice of instrument was Pat Martino, who went through a succession of PAF L5s in both its Venetian and Florentine cutaway variants. George Benson, Jack Wilkins, Ted Dunbar, and Warren Nunes were just a few of the notable one-time players of PAF L5CES'.

Warren Nunes

Jack Wilkins

THE L5CT PLAYERS

By far the best known L5CT player was Hank Garland, whose JAZZ WINDS FROM A NEW DIRECTION (Columbia Cl1572) influenced the likes of George Benson, Bucky Barrett, Lenny Breau, Tony Caldwell and countless others during the early 60s. Garland's fleet bebop lines were played on a 1959 L5CT (serial number A30620) through a Gibson G A 77 amplifier. Garland's distinctive full, yet biting, sound was created in part by the unique combination of a thinner-bodied guitar and the installation of a, 1930s style, Charlie Christian pickup. Heavy roundwound strings, a 15 inch speaker and Garland's dextrous articulation were also major contributing factors to the wonderful sound he produced on JAZZ WINDS FROM A NEW DIRECTION.

Unlike the production models of the L5CT, Garland's instrument was finished in sunburst and fitted with a full (25 ½") scale fingerboard. The optional Charlie Christian pickup (Gibson fitted these to several Gobels) was fitted at Garland's express request because he liked the sound of a beat-up 1930s ES150 he had purchased from a Nashville taxi cab driver. Garland had also fitted Christians to his L7C and his "Byrdland" prototype.

Other well known L5CT players included Billy Byrd, Steve Jordan, Turk Van Lake and, of course, George Gobel.

Hank Garland practicing at home in 1958 with a prototype Byrdland guitar (serial # A20470). Notice that the original L5 tailpiece has been changed.

inset:
George Gobel from 1962 catalogue with the Super 400 which engulfed him!

Grant Geisman playing his 1968 Gibson L5 with Chuck Mangione at the taping for the "Is It Live or Is It Memorex?" television commercial, circa 1978.

CHAPTER 7

Transition

The years between 1965 and 1969 were a period of transition for Gibson. The so-called "beat boom" resulted in a dramatic increase in the sales of electric guitars which enabled the company to both expand its Parsons Street plant, and to introduce a variety of new models.

While this increased demand applied primarily to thinline semi-acoustic and solid bodied guitars, production of the L5CES remained steady but dipped noticeably in 1965 and 1966 as can be seen from the following shipping totals:

L5 Shipping Totals - 1965-1969

	1965	1966	1967	1968	1969
L5CES	34	23	102	189	170
L5CESN	10	1	5	11	55
L5C	15	25	10	36	70
L5CN	1	9	0	3	19

Production of the L5C was, by contrast, significantly down between 1965 and 1967. By 1968 the company had dramatically stepped up its overall output and even the anachronistic L5C almost tripled its previous years shipping totals.

As Gibson increased its production, the management strove to further expand the company's profit margins. The main focus, it seems, was on finding ways of making mass production less labour intensive and therefore more cost effective. But, whilst this may have led to greater consistency across the board, in many instances cost cutting resulted in the "tail wagging the dog." In other words, rather than the manufacturing operations being determined by a particular instrument's design specifications, the instrument was redesigned to accommodate a number of more economical manufacturing processes.

If, for example, reducing the size of pickguards meant that several could be cut simultaneously, then a size reduction would be made regardless of any deviation from the original design. Consequently, several important changes in specifications and components can be attributed to the ethos of increased profit through the intensification of mass production.

Changes In Specifications and Components

In an attempt to increase productivity, to meet the rapidly escalating demand for electric guitars, Gibson's executives reappraised each of the company's manufacturing techniques in turn. From the outset they found that many of the traditional labour intensive operations could be easily automated with the concomitant reduction in labour costs.

Before they could implement this automation, however, some of the components and construction specifications had to be changed.

Of course, there were other factors which influenced manufacturing policy, some of which were, indirectly, "public-led." One such instance was the change of headstock rake which began with the solids and then rapidly spread across the entire range. The angle at which the headstock sloped away from the neck was reduced from 17 to 14 degrees during the closing months of 1965 as a result of the high incidence of headstock breakages on solid bodied guitars. This alteration was not overtly related to increased productivity, although it did mean that less timber was required for each neck.

Additionally, between 1965 and 1969 both the profile of the necks, and nut widths, of the L5Cs and CES', lacked consistency. Necks of the electric models, in particular, became noticeably narrower and had a more rounded profile. A number of L5CES' were made, on a non-custom order basis, with necks no more than an inch wide at the nut. Such instruments were in marked contrast to the early Florentine cutaway L5CES, which had a wider fingerboard and flatter contour to the back of the neck. It is not uncommon, therefore, to find L5CES' from this period which have been completely re-necked.

The L5C, on the other hand, appears to have maintained sensible dimensions, albeit somewhat slimmer and rounder than those found on pre 1965 models.

The next structural change took place midway through 1969, when the Florentine cutaway on the CES was phased out. By reverting to its earlier Venetian style cutaway, the CES was able to utilize the same rims, tops and backs (up to the point of strutting) as its acoustic counterpart. Eradicating the necessity to produce two body shapes for what was essentially the same guitar (the initial manufacturing operations were common to both instruments) saved time and money.

The company could also make the decision as to whether an L5 would be a C or a CES at a later point in its construction, thereby providing greater flexibility for matching L5s with incoming orders. The 1969 Venetian cutaway was subtly different from the earlier version in that it was less gradual and featured a marked dip directly in line with the top of the pickguard. This deviation from the earlier, more open, style first appeared on the L5C, during the mid 60s.

A transitional L5C with revised Venetian cutaway

By the time the Florentine cutaway was discontinued, the company had changed hands and the new owners, NORLIN, went on to make yet further structural changes to both L5s during the 1970s.

The last structural change, excepting of course the phasing out of plywood backs on the CES, concerned the size and shape of the headstocks. As Gibson's headstocks grew increasingly larger, in 1968/9, the headstock of both L5s was noticeably reduced in size. Gibson's use of larger headstocks was, for reasons now unknown, a market ploy to increase the visibility of the name and consequently the brand of guitar being used. Paradoxically the L5, long established as a Gibson "flagship," was not given this treatment. Perhaps the management decided that the extra binding, coupled with the time and care needed to produce a larger headstock on such an ornate model, outweighed the perceived advantages.

We should also remember that, comparatively speaking, L5s were made in relatively small numbers, and were, therefore, unlikely to be seen as frequently as Les Pauls, 335s and SGs.

Finishes

Despite the addition of gold in 1952 (ES295), black in 1954 (Les Paul Custom) and cherry red in 1959 (ES335, George Gobel, etc.) Gibson's L5 standard finishes throughout the transitional period continued to be sunburst and natural. The colour of the sunburst, however, was to change considerably during the course of 1969.

While it was true of say that Gibson never actually attained a standard form of sunburst, the 1969 finish was (for the L5 at any rate), a significant departure from the traditional archtop styling.

Previous L5 sunbursts had ranged from the two-toned dark Cremona (1925-1955) to the three-tone graduated brown/red/yellow finishes (1956-68), all of which in themselves differed markedly from year to year, and shipment to shipment. The year 1969 saw the migration of the light cherry sunburst from the Barney Kessel and Les Paul Deluxe to the Florentine cutaway L5CES. This finish was then retained for the reinstatement of the Venetian cutaway L5CES, and continued to be used for this model up until the mid to late '70s when, due to popular appeal, two additional sunbursts (tobacco sunburst and vintage sunburst) were introduced.

Front and back of 1969 cherry sunburst L5CES

The pale cherry finish was much paler than previous sunbursts and there was a noticeable absence of the archtops' "traditional" brown and yellow hues. This altogether lighter form of sunburst was also used for the Super 400 CES over the same period of time. Additionally some L5Cs, Super 400Cs, Johnny Smiths and Byrdlands were also finished in cherry sunburst, although the colours varied to such an extent that it would be difficult to generalize as to precisely which finish represented the standard form of the sunburst on these models during the transition period.

Components

As well as the previously discussed evolutionary structural changes, the L5 acquired some new components during its transitional period. The pickguard, for example, was shortened and fastened to the top of the instrument with a simple downward screw, replacing the long established neck pinning system. This method of affixing the pickguard to the top of the guitar had actually been introduced around 1960 for the L5CES, but was not used for its acoustic counterpart until the mid 60s. Similarly the L5C continued to utilize a longer pickguard until the late sixties, when one assumes the company's management would have questioned the necessity of fabricating and stocking two different sizes.

The next change in components applied only to the L5CES, in that it concerned the replacement of the gold-capped control knobs. These were phased out during the last few months of 1965 and beginning of 1966, when they were replaced by wide rimmed "sombrero" knobs. The central posts of these black plastic knobs were vertically ridged to enhance grip, while the wide flat rims carried the numbers one to ten. The raised metal pointers, previously mounted on washers beneath the gold capped bonnet knobs, were no longer necessary and, therefore, discarded. "Sombrero" knobs, like their predecessors, were also gold capped, although the caps themselves were smaller in diameter and had a brushed matt as opposed to shiny, appearance.

sombrero knobs were introduced
during the course of 1966

Despite these changes, and perhaps in part because of them, the popularity of both forms of L5 began to wane.

The shipping totals for Gibson's "transitional" period (1965-69) clearly show an increasing preference for electric L5s. And, even though the number of L5Cs produced in 1969, was up on the number produced in 1959 (excluding the L5CT), the annual shipment of 89 L5Cs, as compared to 225 CES' revealed an ominous trend. By 1973/4 annual shipments of the L5C were below double figures and Gibson's long tradition in the art of archtop lutherie was soon to be all but completely overshadowed by Norlin's clamour to produce more and more Les Pauls.

Transitional L5CES

Transitional L5C and CES Players

Many of those who played PAF L5CES' were later to use transitional models. Pat Martino, George Benson, Ted Dunbar and, of course, Wes Montgomery fall into this category.

Gibson made two custom L5Cs in 1965 for Wes Montgomery. They were basically hybrids not strictly speaking new instruments but ones which utilized a combination of features from the L5C and CES. Both guitars had single, patent number, humbuckers in the neck position with tone and volume controls between the treble "F" hole and the bridge. The pickguards were pinned to the side of the neck similar to those of the contemporary L5C but, unlike the C, both of the guitars had metal tune-o-matic bridges, while their basic construction was almost certainly transitional. For example the cutaways on both instruments had the pre 1965 "open" profile yet the angle of the headstocks utilized the 1965 14 degree rake. Both guitars were also fitted with shiny gold capped bonnet knobs at a time when they were being officially phased out.

Both of Montgomery's single pickup L5CES' did have a unique feature, however, and that was the addition of a decorative mother-of-pearl inlay on the upper treble bout.

This, on first appearance, aesthetic decoration was in actual fact purposely added to protect the instrument from Montgomery's fingernails, which had worn through the wood on an earlier L5!

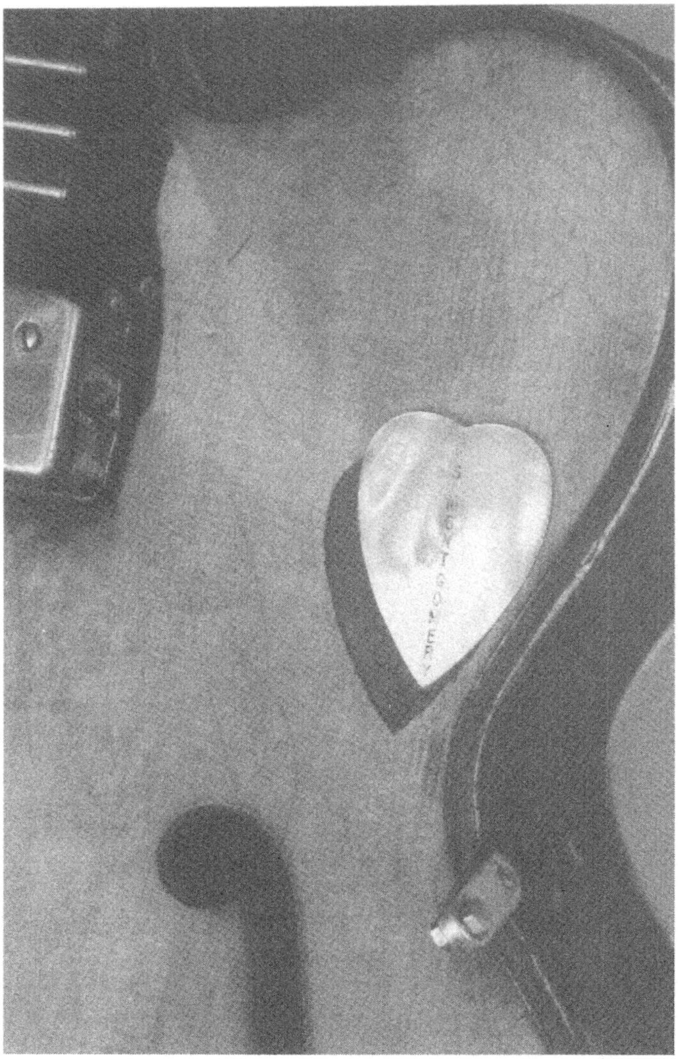

Detail of one of Montgomery's single pickup L5CES' damaged in a fire. This one has the mother-of-pearl inlay with Wes's name.

Following Montgomery's untimely death in 1968, the L5CES grew far less visible. Its status was, of course, perpetuated, by association, on a number of LP sleeves, as continues to be the case today.

Yet while there was no real "biggy" playing the instrument exclusively after Wes' death, the L5CES was still the trusty workhorse of numerous gifted jazz guitarists, such as Pat Martino, Vic Juris, Richie Hart and Jack Wilkins. So too was the L5C, a great favourite with studio guitarists on account of its ability to function as either an acoustic or an electric guitar. For the older generation of session players like Don Arnone, Tony Mottola, Remo Palmier and Danny Perri (USA) and Ike Isaacs, Roland Harker and Terry Walsh (UK) the L5C was still the first choice of instrument.

Wes Montgomery with the "Working Man's Guitar" from Gibson advertisement

Ike Isaacs with mid 60's L5C (changed tuners)

Louis Stewart with transitional L5CES

Richie Hart with L5CES

Herb Ellis with Florentine cutaway L5CESN

Pat Martino (1975)

Wes Montgomery from the Historic Collection Catalog

Trefor Owen with mid 60s L5CES (changed control knobs)

CHAPTER 8

The Norlin Years

Gibson's period of transition lasted roughly between 1965 and 1970. It was a time when, without exception, Gibson guitars departed from the revered and established traditions of the 1940s and 50s, and evolved into instruments which appeared to have less soul and personality.

There had, of course, been many fundamental changes in specifications, methods of construction, hardware and even the subtle nuances of coloring. Inevitably such changes soon led to a belief amongst players and collectors alike that Gibson no longer represented a pinnacle of the guitar manufacturing industry; that they had somehow slipped from the position of pre-eminence they deservedly maintained for so long.

While this trend began during the mid 60s, following the resignations of Ted McCarty (President) and John Huis (Vice President), it did not reach its zenith until the mid to late seventies, when Gibson was experiencing the consequences of several years under the control of Norlin.

On December the 19th, 1969 CMI sold 96% of its shares in Gibson to ECL Industries. By 1970, ECL had changed its name to Norlin and was to manage the finances and policy making for the manufacture and sales of Gibson guitars until the 15th of January 1986.

During this period, an increased focus upon productivity, and continuous push for greater profit margins, resulted in a number of measures which had a serious effect upon the quality and consistency of the end product. In short, Norlin unwittingly created a legacy of dubious and, at best, inconsistent quality control which left a lasting blight upon the trade name.

While this sad situation was never intentionally premeditated, it did nevertheless reflect both a profound disregard for Gibson's long tradition and a seriously misguided perception of the market.

Fortunately, since 1986 the strength of Gibson's name alone has been marketed in such a way as to allow valuable ground to be regained. Indeed, the current owners show a depth of understanding and commitment which represents a marked contrast to the Norlin ethos and has consequently enabled them to move forward in a more positive way.

Norlin, on the other hand, were obsessed with profit and manufacturing efficiency, ruthlessly cutting their costs with little regard for the consequences.

Gibson's eventual relocation in Nashville, Tennessee was, in itself, a result of these cost cutting measures. The new facility, on Elm Pike Lane, was opened in 1975 and the production of instruments gradually stepped up until the original Kalamazoo plant was decomissioned in July 1984.

Solid bodied guitars in general, and Les Pauls in particular, became the main centre of focus at the new plant. By the late 70s, the production of Gibson's semi-acoustic range (ES335, 345, 347, etc.) had also been transferred to Nashville. Although full bodied instruments such as the ES175 and Howard Roberts Artist and Custom continued to be made, the main body of craftsmen responsible for the various L5, Super 400 and Johnny Smith models chose to remain in Kalamazoo.

By the early 80s, Gibson had reached a low ebb in the traditional art of archtop lutherie and, perhaps more seriously, only a handful of employees with the necessary skills and experience to build these instruments remained on the payroll.

Norlin L5CESN

If Gibson's transitional period marked the departure from long established methods and materials, it was the ensuing years under Norlin's direction which consolidated the ethos of profit before product.

Change had previously been evolutionary, as the majority of new practices and procedures had been introduced on an ad hoc basis. Norlin's approach on the other hand was to aggressively seek out methods of increasing output whilst decreasing outlay. Automation was stepped up, raw materials were re-sourced and cheaper hardware was introduced. Many of these measures, although not all, were to have a tangible effect upon the production quality of the L5C and L5CES.

The first economy was essentially a preventative measure, designed to reduce the increasing amount of warranty work. Since 1968, and the reintroduction of the single cutaway Les Paul, Gibson had received a steady stream of complaints about headstock breakages. The weight of Les Pauls in particular meant that if the guitar toppled over, the headstock was likely to fracture behind the nut. Gibson's first reaction was to reduce the angle of the headstock pitch, but even that modification was found to offer little protection on the heavier guitars.

In late 1969, the Research and Design team came up with an apparently viable solution. An additional mass of timber was retained, at the acute point of curvature, to form a semi-circular heel. Although this additional bulk strengthened the curve to such an extent that it eventually allowed Gibson to revert back to the 14 degree headstock rake, it was an aesthetic disaster. Volutes, as these conspicuous heels came to be known, proved extremely unpopular, not only for their unGibsonlike appearance, but also for their cumbersome bulky feel. Nevertheless volutes quickly spread throughout the range and continued to be used until 1981/82.

Coinciding with the arrival of the volute came another departure from a long established tradition. The black peghead fascia, which had previously been made from a soft white wood (holly), was replaced by a cheaper and more workable composite fibre. This new material enabled fascias to be mass produced more readily, while at the same time, facilitated greater speed and efficiency in the inlaying of motifs and logos. Gibson claimed that the new material was introduced expressly to prevent surface cracking or lacquer checking as it is sometimes called. This seems unlikely for when such surface cracking did take place it was invariably in the upper layers of the cellulose lacquer, and while wood shrinkage may have been a contributing factor, the cellulose overspray still remained susceptible to climatic extremes.

At the same time as these new fascias were introduced, the design of the mother-of-pearl, flowerpot inlay was modified and reduced in size. This change, was made to coincide with the arrival of the fibre veneers and was purposely designed to eradicate a number of "hands on" and time consuming operations.

By 1970, the wide rimmed truss rod cover, synonymous with Gibson's premier instruments such as the L5, Byrdland and Johnny Smith, was abandoned. In its place, Norlin utilized the regular, and much plainer, cover which was already fitted, as standard, to most other models. The adoption of a "common" trussrod cover constituted a significant saving, in that it once again reduced the inventory of parts. In order to differentiate between the various guitars, however, the model name, or number, was subsequently engraved on the trussrod cover. In the case of both L5s, the engraved designation was the same- "CUSTOM L5".

Although cosmetic, this change was indicative of Norlin's disregard for those small, but important, aesthetic details on which the Gibson tradition had been built.

Norlin introduced further changes to both L5s during the course of 1970. The metal foot and riser block, which affixed the pickguard to the rim of the guitar, was replaced by a simple bent metal bracket. Instead of passing through a plastic riser block, hidden discretely beneath the pickguard, the metal bracket was fastened to the pickguard via a gold-plated nut and bolt, the head of which was clearly visible, through the top of the pickguard. The pickguard itself was also mounted further back from the cutaway than it had been on the earlier (circa 1939-70 Cs and 1951-61 CES') Venetian cutaway models.

Like the new trussrod covers, the metal brackets were common to other models in the electro-acoustic range. They were easier to fit, had fewer constituent parts, and did not require the same degree of precision engineering as the former foot, rod, nut and cap configuration.

Because the foot and riser block fitting had been standard on Gibson L5s since their introduction, the new bracket was perceived as a significant "downgrade", despite the fact that similar brackets had been used in the 40s on various mandolins, and since the 50s on single cutaway Les Pauls. Perhaps it was because by that time the simple bent brackets were synonymous with budget instruments, such as the ES120, ES125 and ES140, that they appeared rather incongruous on such a high quality guitar as the L5. Nevertheless, these brackets were used right up until 1993, when the post-Norlin owners introduced their so-called "Historic Collection" and reverted back to the traditional riser block and foot arrangement.

Paradoxically, while the new bracket reduced the company's inventory of parts, Norlin's next modification, embossing the company logo into the pickup covers, increased it. Following this move, the outer covers of humbucking pickups were no longer interchangeable. The person/s responsible for the idea had, apparently, failed to realize that the neck and bridge pickups would require separate covers in order to avoid showing the logo upside down. As a direct consequence of the subsequent and unexpected additional cost incurred by doubling everyone's inventory requirements, the idea was quickly dropped and the embossed covers duly phased out. By 1973, these covers were no longer used. They were still available separately as spares, but ceased to be fitted on new instruments leaving the factory. During the mid 70s Norlin introduced two new colour options in an attempt to revitalize the flagging sales of its semi-acoustic and full-bodied guitars. By 1976, Cherry and Black had been added to the existing choices of Sunburst and Blonde. These opaque colors had the additional advantage of masking the plain grained timbers which were increasingly utilized for all of the company's premium quality instruments.

Norlin's confidence in the Gibson name, and belief that the public would continue to buy despite downgrades in materials, cosmetics and workmanship, resulted in an almost blase attitude which was reflected in the quality of their products. Even the natural finish L5s, which retained their higher price on account of the necessity to use figured woods, were leaving the factory with non-existent figuring or, at best, woods which resembled speckled balsa!

On sunburst models, the gradual build-up of nitro-cellulose coloring was reduced by the introduction of an alcohol based rubbing stain. The resulting "antique" sunburst, which was initially intended for the ES300 thinlines, was soon carried over to a wide variety of instruments including L5s, Super 400s, ES175s and Byrdlands.

Running concurrently with the introduction of these new finishes were two changes of machineheads. The first, which took place during the late seventies, can be identified by a screw-headed bolt which passed directly through the tuning button and secured it to the shaft. These were replaced, during the early 80s, by machineheads with retractable cranks in the tuning buttons, purposely designed for speedy string changing. This ingenious, if novel, idea proved unpopular, particularly on the deep bodied guitars, and Gibson duly returned to the Kluson shaped machineheads with the central retaining bolt. Like an increasing number of metal components for a variety of Gibson guitars, both types of machineheads were manufactured by Schaller.

Other models

During the 70s, several new models were introduced which borrowed, in one way or another, from the Venetian cutaway L5CES. Paradoxically, the guitar which had the most fitments and features in common with the L5CES, was also the most radically different.

The L5S, introduced in late 1972 and first shipped in 1973, was marketed as a solid-bodied version of the L5CES. In keeping with its larger cousin, the L5S was placed in the top-of-the-range, premium instrument price bracket and, as such, adopted most of the decorative adornments associated with full-bodied L5s. There were, of course significant differences. The L5S did not, for example, have "F" holes or a pickguard, which in turn reduced the instrument's overall level of ornamentation. The 7-ply top and 3 ply back binding, together with the characteristic L5 headstock motif, were retained, as was the art deco tailpiece. Yet, despite these obvious similarities, the size and shape, together with the resulting feel and weight, were markedly different.

Gibson's plan, to offer a scaled down solid bodied version of the L5CES, was fraught with problems. Creating the same body and cutaway profile, for example, on an instrument which had been reduced in size from seventeen to thirteen and a half inches proved difficult, and the eventual shape, while similar in some respects to the Venetian cutaway L5CES, was not quite the miniature replica that Gibson had anticipated.

There were three basic variants of the L5S, the first and arguably most attractive, was to prove the least successful, largely because of its low impedance pickups. Developed in 1969, by Les Paul, and fitted initially to his self-named Les Paul Personal and Professional and subsequently to the Les Paul Recording and Signature models, low impedance pickups were an unqualified flop, despite of their quieter performance and resulting advantages for studio work.

Unlike the pickups fitted to the aforementioned guitars, those used for the L5S had gold plated covers, to match the instrument's tailpiece, bridge and tuners. To further support the opulent L5 theme the same tailpiece as that fitted to the contemporaneous L5CES and L5C was used which enabled the company to draw from existing stocks. The bridge, however, was screwed to the body in a similar manner to those found on the various Les Pauls and ES300s, while the bridge saddles were the recently developed wide-travel variety; a new idea which necessitated a bulkier housing. This new "oversized" bridge became known as the Nashville bridge on account of its close association with many of the new models, originating from Tennessee. (Les Paul Signature, Les Paul Recording, SI, L6-S, Marauder, ES325 etc.)

The second variant of the L5S appeared towards the close of 1974, and the main difference between this model and its predecessor was the gold-plated humbuckers which were introduced to replace the, unpopular, low impedance pickups. Cosmetically, at least, this change brought the L5S closer in line with the L5CES.

The third and final variant of the L5S is readily identifiable by the absence of its extended art deco tailpiece. During the course of late 1975 and early 1976, the heavy L5 tailpiece was changed to the simpler (and less costly) "stop" tailpiece which was already fitted to the majority of Gibson's solid-bodied guitars.

Apparently this change, which overtly reduced the similarity between the L5S and L5CES, was introduced in order to increase sustain. Whatever the company's alleged reason for this change, it was in retrospect "public led," for the mid-seventies marked a period of intense controversy about the pros and cons of bolted (stop) versus floating (archtop) tailpieces. As the decade progressed, public opinion virtually forced the company to re-introduce "stop" tailpieces on instruments which had not used them since the mid sixties.

Ironically, by 1978 the simple stop tailpiece had also been changed, in favor of the TP6.

L5S Players

Despite having an uninterupted production run which outlasted any other Gibson solid, with the exception of the Les Paul, the L5S had few notable champions.

Its best known player was undoubtedly Pat Martino, who used the model, albeit for a short period, during the mid-seventies. Martino's affinity with Gibson solid-bodied guitars stemmed from his early teens, when he paid his dues on his father's gold top Les Paul Standard. He particularly like the Les Paul because of its compact size, and it is likely that he decided to play an L5S for the same reason

The L5S he chose was a cherry sunburst, second variant model, with a moderately flamed three-piece top. As with his archtops, Martino strung the L5S with very heavy gauge strings (circa 17 to 58): The extended L5 tailpiece and Bulky "wide travel" bridge would most certainly have helped to stabilize the instrument under the tremendous tension exerted by such heavy strings.

Like any other guitar in Pat's hands, the L5S sounded full, warm and incisive as can be evidenced on his classic Warner Brothers album JOYUS LAKE (BS 2977).

Despite its apparent suitability for the jazz idiom, and similarity to its full bodied counterpart, the L5S was never really adopted as a "legitimate" jazz guitar.

Other jazzers to play it, however, did include Billy Butler, who had an early model with low impedence pickups, and Clint Strong, who currently plays a third variant L5S with the stop tailpiece and, unusually, a regular tune-o-matic bridge.

Surprisingly, considering its versatility and "trademark" Gibson tone, the L5S was not a huge success with rock and pop guitarists either. Paul Simon played one for a while during the late 70s and early 80s as did Kevin Peek who used a second variant model with John William's supergroup SKY. The best known rock guitarist to use the L5S, however, was undoubtedly Keith Richards who, even now, occasionally plays a stop tailpiece model with an atypical black finish.

Besides the L5S, Norlin introduced a further two models which took their inspiration from the L5. Launched in 1978 the Super V CES, and its acoustic counterpart the Super V BJB, were basically hybrids; borrowing features from both the L5 and Super 400.

Pat Martino in Nashville in 1976

Clint Strong with L5S

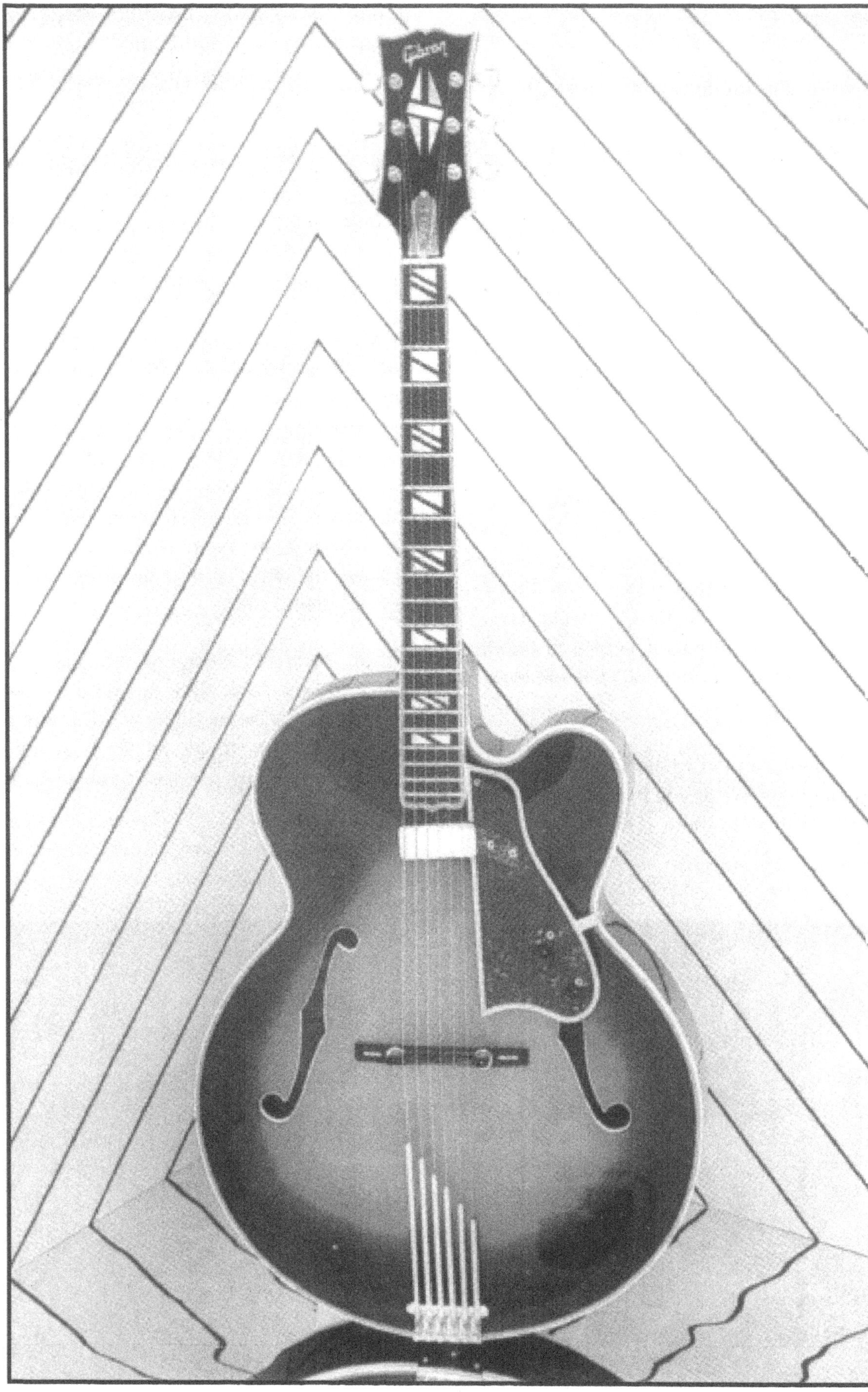

Super V BJB

The Super V CES was essentially an L5CES with a Super 400 neck and headstock. One feature, however, which set the Super Vs apart from L5s and Super 400s was the new, for that year, 6 finger adjustable tailpiece. Despite selling in small numbers and never finding its way into the hands of a really well known player, the Super V CES is still catalogued.

Conversely, the acoustic Super V BJB (so called because it came equipped with a Bruce J Bolan floating pickup) was only made between 1978 and 1984.

While neither of these instruments attracted well known players, they have nevertheless been used by some very good guitarists such as Mike Elliott, Robert Yelin, Steve Laury, David Smith and Bruce Clarke.

David Smith with Super V BJB

Robert Yelin with Super V CES

Norlin L5 Players

Many of the second and third generation bebop guitarists play the Norlin L5CES model on account of its suitability for the genre, and its relative cost.

When the price of earlier examples began to spiral as, a result of the burgeoning collectors' market, the gigging guitarist was forced to seek alternatives. The prohibitive asking prices, for example, of 50s and early 60s L5CES' meant that the confirmed "Gibsonite" and "would be" L5 player was limited to less desirable L5s,such as non-cutaway acoustics and CES models from the 1970s.

Some players chose other brands like Guild and Epiphone, or handmade instruments from the proliferation of independent luthiers; but a number of guitarists remained loyal to the brand name and purchased L5CES' made during the 1970s. One of the best known, and most highly regarded of these players is Peter Leitch.

Leitch purchased his 1972 L5CESN, serial number 72558133, in 1980 from a music store in Toronto. He first used it on the 25th August 1980 and it was his main guitar up until December 1992, when it was seriously damaged in an accident. Leitch continues the story:

"I bought the L5 in August 1980 from a music store in Toronto, Canada. I have been told that it was built in 1971 or 1972 and it was in almost mint condition. It seems to me I paid $1200 CDN for it, but there was also an amplifier involved in some kind of trade.

I first used the instrument on a gig on August 25th, 1980, with trumpeter Kenny Wheeler at Toronto's Bourbon Street Club. I remember the date well, because that night I met my wife!

I played the L5 almost exclusively from then on, until the accident. After travelling the world (Russia, Europe, Australia, all over North America) for about 15 years with the instrument in a soft gig bag, without incident, I dropped it on my living room floor one morning in December 1992. The instrument is repairable but it looks like an expensive job."

Leitch strung the L5 with D'Addarios in the unusually light gauges of 10, 13, 18 (wound) 26, 36 and 46. Apart from removing the pickguard and replacing the black sombrero knobs with hatbox knobs from 2, single pickup, P90 175s, he made no further modifications.

Following the L5's unfortunate collision with the living room floor, Leitch now plays a Framus Atilla Zoller (model A Z Award) but the sound of his Norlin L5CES can be heard on no less than thirteen albums.

Peter Leitch

Joshua Breakstone is, another contemporary bebop guitarist rapidly making a name for himself. Having played and recorded with such jazz luminaries as Barry Harris, Tommy Flanagan, Jack McDuff and Pepper Adams, Breakstone is already considered by many to be a major figure in the jazz world.

Like Leitch, Breakstone plays an early 70s Norlin L5CES but in a sunburst rather than natural finish. In fact he likes the instrument so much that he has purchased a second "backup" L5CES from the same period.

Coincidentally the pickguards on both L5s had crystallized and were removed to avoid cellulose oxidization discoloring the finish, but apart from this, both instruments are "stock".

Breakstone strings his L5s with Ernie Ball medium light nickel wounds gauges 12, 16, 24, 32, 44, 54.

Other notable jazz players, closely associated with Norlin L5s include Royce Campbell, Calvin Keys, Roland Prince, and Joe Cohn (USA), Heiner Franz and Joe Bawelino (Germany), Franco Cerri (Italy) and Jean Pierre LLabador (France).

Several rock guitarists have also used them, the best known of which are probably Andy Summers, Lou Reed and Paul Rodgers.

Joe Bowelion

Royce Campbell with a cherry finish Norlin L5CES

Heiner Franz

J Pierre Llabador

Calvin Keyes

Joe Cohn

CHAPTER 9

Rejuvenation

On January 15th, 1986 following seven months of intensive negotiations, Norlin sold the Gibson Guitar Company to a trio of young and successful entrepreneurs. The sale ushered in a crucial period of rejuvenation. Just several months away from potential liquidation, the company was saved and eventually "turned around" by Henry Juszkiewicz, David Berryman and Gary Zebrowski. Zebrowski took a back seat and eventually switched his energies to Phil Technologies, so his association with Gibson thereafter was primarily as a stockholder.

Henry Juszkiewicz was the principal driving force behind the trio's decision to purchase the ailing company. Engineering experience acquired whilst working for General Motors, and a business acumen sharpened by stints at Rochester and Harvard Universities, furnished Juszkiewicz with the ideal background for directorship of a musical instrument manufacturing company.

More importantly, since playing in a number of "garage" bands during his teens, Juszkiewcz had been an avid enthusiast of Gibson guitars.

After purchasing the company, a dramatic yet common sense reorganization quickly followed. With Juszkiewicz as Chairman and Berryman as President, the quality of Gibson guitars gradually improved to a level comparable with Kalamazoo's best. Care, control, consistency and a creative blend of computer and hands-on manufacturing techniques resulted in a consumer confidence which even the most optimistic of "Gibsonites" thought would be impossible to regain.

By hiring employees who play or have a real interest in the guitar, and reintroducing many of Gibson's "classic" models, such as the Citation, Tal Farlow and L5CES, Gibson has regained the respect of older players, whilst at the same time established a strong position in the current market.

One of Juszkiewicz's undoubtable successes has been the meticulously produced vintage reissue series, on which all of the Historical Collection 1934 reissues are based.

1989 L5CES

1990 L5CES

Three new L5s including a rare natural Wes Montgomery model

No less than three L5s are included in this ambitious collection of reissues: a 1934 Non-cutaway, non-advanced model, a so-called 1951 L5CES and a Wes Montgomery single pickup model. Whilst beautifully made, with the highest quality timbers and craftsmanship, these L5s do, however, deviate from their original specifications.

1934 L5 Non-cutaway

As a replica of the original, the HISTORIC COLLECTION 1934 L5 is an attractive and convincing guitar. It does, however, differ in several ways from the real thing. The headstock of the original was slimmer, more tapered and had rather more pronounced dips a the top. The positioning of the 19th fret, in relationship to the end of the fingerboard, was also different.

Matching present day parts with the earlier, obsolete ones, has always been a problem, evident here in the tuning buttons which were originally a different shape and flatter; the truss rod cover which should be unbound (non laminated) and the rosewood bridge, which should be ebony and not compensated.

Because of the intensive "hands on" nature of their construction, L5s built during the 1930s tended to differ in aspects of fine detail; no two instruments were identical. This posed something of a problem for the HISTORIC COLLECTION; which particular guitar should be copied?

After closely examining several guitars from the period, an exceptionally fine example of a 1934 L5 (serial number 91908) from the Tom Van Hoose Collection was chosen, and it was this particular instrument (depicted in color plate 17 of Van Hoose's Super 400 Book)* on which all of the HISTORIC COLLECTION L5 reissues are based.

* ***"Gibson Super 400- Art of the Fine Guitar"***

Gibson's 1934 Historic Collection L5

1951 L5 CES

The differences between this reissue and the original 1951 L5CES are too many to list. In essence the HISTORIC COLLECTION L5CES is a modern version based, not upon a 1951 model, but on the relatively small numbers of L5CES' produced during the 80s and 90s.

It represents a continuation of tradition rather than a specific replica from a given point in time. Indeed, there are a number of confusing anachronisms such as the mid 50s bonnet knobs, the 40s style engraving on the tailpiece, and the 70s bolt fastening tuning pegs and narrow-edged truss rod cover. Add to this the reissue 1957 humbuckers and late 60s ebony tune-o-matic and it becomes difficult to envisage how this guitar could be accurately called 'historic' or a reissue. Nevertheless, it is a current production L5CES, and as such looks to the future as much as it does to the past. If Gibson intends to marry the best of the past with the best of the future, as evidenced on many of its current instruments the HISTORIC COLLECTION L5CES can only be seen as a successful blend of old and new.

The Wes Montgomery

Essentially a single pickup L5CES, this model is not actually listed as an L5, although it does share the same designated truss rod cover as the aforementioned 1951 L5CES. Similarly, there are anachronisms and inaccuracies which militate against the WES MONTGOMERY as a precise replica of Wes' mid 60s single pickup L5CES'.

The ebony base tune-o-matic bridge, uncapped bonnet knobs and method of fastening the pickguard to the top of the guitar all differ. Furthermore, the distinctive mother-of-pearl inlays, which characterized the tops of Wes' guitars, are also missing. Instead his name is engraved on the silver tailpiece insert. Again the WES MONTGOMERY should not be viewed strictly as a reissue, but more as a modern day equivalent of an earlier and extremely rare guitar.

Archtop authority/historian Tom Van Hoose must be given some of the credit for the inclusion of this particular model in the HISTORIC COLLECTION. It was his persistent requests for such an instrument which led Jim Triggs and Tom Murphy to test the waters of commercial viability by unveiling a prototype at the 1992 Dallas Show.

As Van Hoose had correctly anticipated, the Wes Montgomery model was extremely well received. This was in no small part due to its attractive price tag as well as its association with Wes. Rather than producing an exact replica of Wes' single pickup L5CES, it was decided to omit the fancy m.o.p. inlays (in the spruce top). Off–the–wall parts, and B–grade spruce were used in order to keep production costs down. This enabled the guitar to be marketed as **the** affordable L5. Indeed, with an initial retail price of $4,500, half the cost of a double pickup L5CES, Gibson has once again made the purchase of an L5 accessible to the player. More importantly, despite its misleading reissue nomenclature, the Wes Montgomery is an intrinsically fine guitar, worthy in every respect of its designated title.

Wes Montgomery L5 (minus pickguard)

Custom Shop L5s

Jim Triggs, Hutch Hutchins, Greg Rich, Terry Ryan and Tom Murphy were amongst the notable luthiers and R + D staff involved, to varying degrees, in Gibson's "custom shop" L5s. These were one off or limited run instruments which ranged from an Emerald green L5CES' with diamond shaped "F" holes (Jim Triggs), to the beautiful 1984 50th Anniversary L5CES (James "Hutch" Hutchins). A limited number of L5Cs, L5CES' with P90 pickups, and L5CTs were also made.

These "custom shop" instruments were all made at the Nashville plant, in a small room adjacent to the ES booth. The pantographic cutting machine for rough carving the top and back plates, rescued from Kalamazoo, ensures that the carved tops of all L5s have a similar contour to the earlier models, while the fine sanding and tap tuning are carried out by hand.

Although the Custom Shop title refers as much to exclusivity as to a designated area of the factory, <u>all</u> current L5s, Super 400s, Citations, Byrdlands and other carved top instruments are made by a small, select, group of luthiers in this specially equipped room.

Four custom shop L5CTs

The Centennial Collection

Strictly limited to a hundred instruments, the CENTENNIAL COLLECTION celebrated Gibson's hundredth anniversary (1894-1994) with panache. Each month during 1994 a different model was produced, all of which had the same luxurious centennial appointments. These included an 11 point diamond on the peghead logo; 5 point diamond detentes on 22K gold plated bonnet knobs; diamond jewelled sterling silver centennial serial number; genuine m.o.p. inlays, including a 12th fret 100th anniversary banner; 22K gold plated centennial Orville Gibson coin, on the back of the headstock, and a hand tooled leather case with protective cover.

Each guitar was supplied with a plethora of accessories, which emphasized their souvenir/collecting and "investment" status.

Silk ribbons, an embossed certificate of authenticity and a jewelled gold signet ring, with personalized 100th anniversary logo, were amongst the celebratory souvenirs which accompanied these guitars.

A small, but undisclosed, number of ebony finish Centennial Collection L5CES' were released during December 1994. With a suggested retail price of $10,000 this "designer" collection was marketed as the ultimate in historical importance: Gibson's most collectable "new" guitars.

L5 Components1986-1995

Excepting the HISTORIC L5s, which strive as far as possible to reproduce the style of earlier obsolete fittings, the L5s produced during the last decade were characterized by a number of small, yet significant changes in hardware. The silver inset in the open central area of the tailpiece, for example was replaced by an oversized wooden applique, carrying a horizontally sloping pearl segment engraved with the designation L5. This change coincided with the introduction of the L4CES (1987) which shared the same tailpiece, albeit without the engraved "L5" designation. Although the "Varitone" adjustment, which had been dropped some years earlier, was still missing, the Varitone's access hole, previously retained for decorative purposes, was dispensed with. In short, the L5's traditional art deco tailpiece became an altogether less complicated affair, with a notable absence of decorative engraving.

Other components also reveal an economy of decoration. The white beveled edge of the truss rod cover became narrower, while the binding of the pickguard was less pronounced. The plastic from which the pickguards were made also changed, from a convincing dark brown imitation tortoiseshell, to a less opaque looking material with a distinctive red tint.

Uncapped bonnet knobs were reintroduced, no doubt drawn from components bulk purchased for Les Pauls. The gold-plated tune-o-matic bridge tops were also replaced by simple uncompensated ebony saddles.

It should be noted, however, that both the above mentioned tailpiece and bridge differ from those fitted to instruments from the HISTORIC COLLECTION.

1990 L5CES

Fitting the endblock

The Players

Whilst there do not appear to be a great many post-Norlin L5s in circulation, several have, nevertheless, found their way into the hands of prominent players. Larry Coryell presently plays both a non-historic collection L5CES and a Wes Montgomery model. He used the latter for his CD *Fallen Angel* and for two tracks on Royce Campbell's *6 X 6* (Paddle Wheel KICJ 220).

Mark Whitfield plays one of the relatively small number of recent issue L5CNs. This instrument, equipped with floating mini-humbucking pickup, is shown on the cover, and inside liner notes, for his CD: *True Blue* (Verve 314 523 591-2).

Other post Norlin L5 players include Don Linke, Lou Mecca, and Sitter Primus.

Sitter Primus

L5 rims and Formers at the Nashville plant

Mark Whitfield

APPENDIX A: *L5 MEMORABILIA*

FAR WES
WES MONTGOMERY
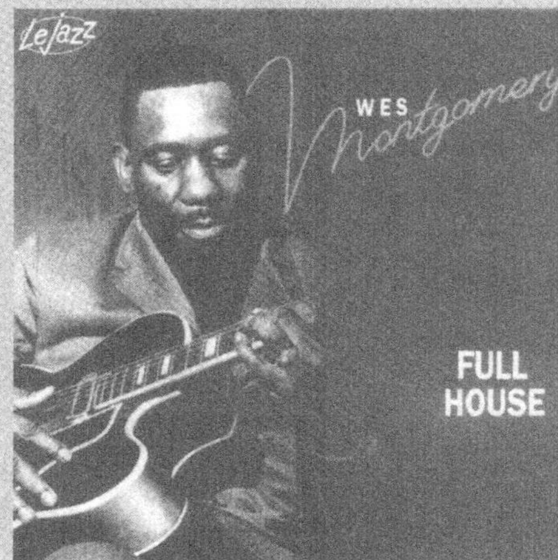
Le Jazz
WES Montgomery
FULL HOUSE

Movin' Wes
Wes Montgomery

PROJECT G-7:
A Tribute to Wes Montgomery
featuring KENNY BURRELL
VOLUME II
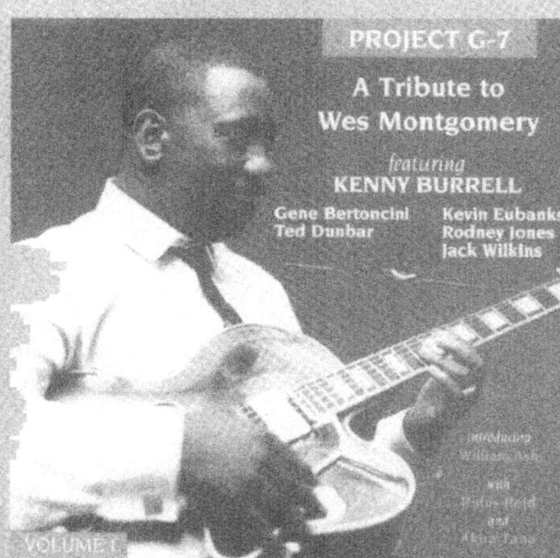
PROJECT G-7
A Tribute to Wes Montgomery
featuring KENNY BURRELL
Gene Bertoncini
Ted Dunbar
Kevin Eubanks
Rodney Jones
Jack Wilkins

HERITAGE
KENNY BURRELL
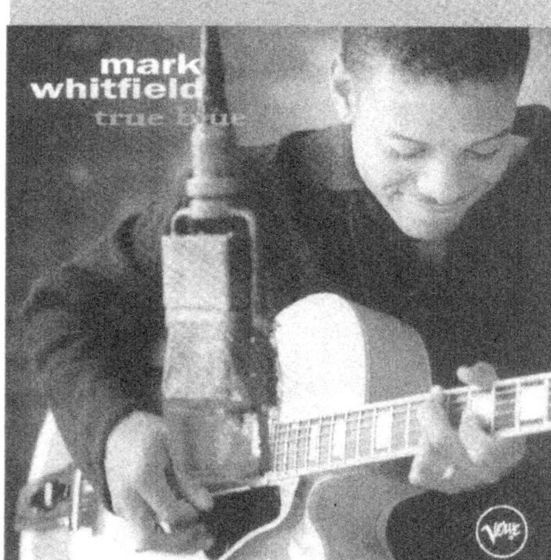
mark whitfield
true blue

Peter Leitch

GENTLE TIME ALONE TED DUNBAR QUARTET
Mickey Tucker, Ray Drummond,
David Jones

Acoustic Guitars
• CARVED TOP MODELS

David Barbour and his GIBSON
An outstanding figure in radio and recording, as well as on stage and screen, David Barbour chooses a Gibson to meet the exacting demands of his busy schedule. He's another on the long roster of famous guitarists who rely on Gibson instruments for smooth response and rich tone to highlight their technique.
Gibson INC.
KALAMAZOO MICHIGAN

Hutch

LOTSA BOSSA NOVA
THE KENNY BURRELL OCTET
GUITARS: KENNY BURRELL, BUCKY PIZZARELLI, BARRY GALBRAITH
BASS: MILT HINTON
DRUMS: OSIE JOHNSON
PERCUSSION WILLY RODRIGUEZ, TOMMY LOPEZ
TENOR SAX AND FLUTE: JEROME RICHARDSON
TRUMPET: CLARK TERRY

1934

Lloyd Loar, designer of the Gibson L-5 non-cutaway

First introduced in 1923, the famed L-5 created an industry standard. Developed by Lloyd Loar's engineering team, the L-5 featured mandolin style f-holes and a graceful 16" body. By 1934 Gibson had enhanced its famed L-5 with elegant appointments such as block pearl inlays, a bound peghead veneer and pickguard. Using a close grained spruce top and solid maple sides and back, the 1934 L-5's distinctive body projects a smooth attack that is welcome in any small ensemble. The 1934 L-5 is the predecessor to other fine instruments and the guitar connoisseur should not consider his collection complete until it includes one of these Historic instruments.

'34 L-5 Non-Cutaway *Cremona Brown Sunburst*

Tuners	**Replica Grover "open back"**
Peghead	**Original "The Gibson" style**
Hardware	**Gold**
Scale /Nut width	**24 ¾" / 1 11/16"**
Fingerboard/Inlay	**Ebony / Block**
Binding	**Body / Neck / Peghead**
Bridge/Tailpiece	**Traditional Rosewood / Trapeze**
Materials	**Figured maple back and sides, Solid spruce top, Three-piece maple neck**
Finish	**Cremona Brown Sunburst**

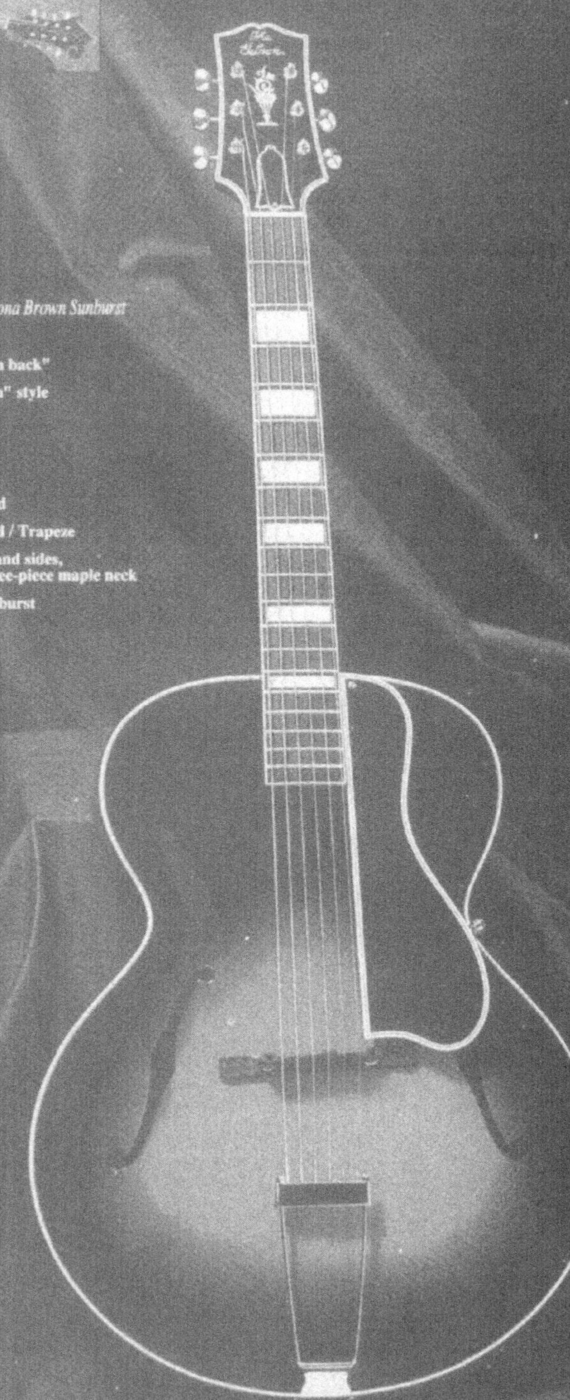

L5 entries from the Historic Collection catalog

1951

In 1951, Gibson answered the huge demand for electric arch top guitars with the introduction of the Super 400 CES. This instrument features a different bracing structure than its precursor, the Super 400 Premier. Strengthened by two long parallel braces with smaller cross bracing, the Super 400 CES provides exactly the right response for its pickups. In production since 1951, the Super 400 CES is as much a part of today's music canvas as it was for master players like Kenny Burrell and Merle Travis. When you bring home a Super 400 CES you bring home history.

Also introduced in 1951, the L-5 CES is both elegant and simple in design. With a hand engraved tailpiece and "torch" peghead inlay, the L-5 CES is a timeless instrument that continues to be an inspiration to modern artists. Uniting a tap-tuned spruce top with maple back and sides, the L-5 CES is a standard which others are judged by and should be included in any serious collection.

L5 entries from the Historic Collection catalog

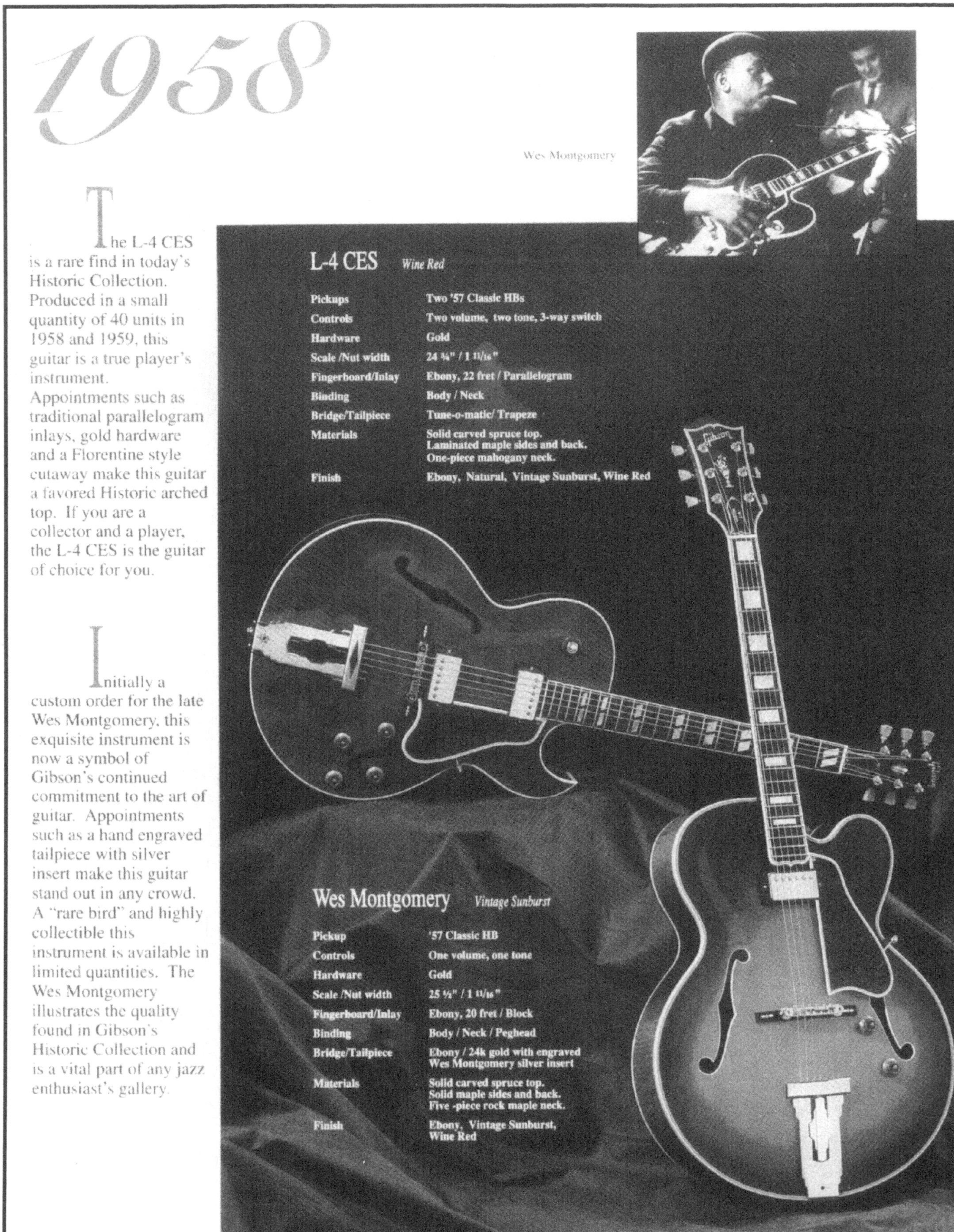

1958

Wes Montgomery

The L-4 CES is a rare find in today's Historic Collection. Produced in a small quantity of 40 units in 1958 and 1959, this guitar is a true player's instrument. Appointments such as traditional parallelogram inlays, gold hardware and a Florentine style cutaway make this guitar a favored Historic arched top. If you are a collector and a player, the L-4 CES is the guitar of choice for you.

Initially a custom order for the late Wes Montgomery, this exquisite instrument is now a symbol of Gibson's continued commitment to the art of guitar. Appointments such as a hand engraved tailpiece with silver insert make this guitar stand out in any crowd. A "rare bird" and highly collectible this instrument is available in limited quantities. The Wes Montgomery illustrates the quality found in Gibson's Historic Collection and is a vital part of any jazz enthusiast's gallery.

L-4 CES *Wine Red*

Pickups	Two '57 Classic HBs
Controls	Two volume, two tone, 3-way switch
Hardware	Gold
Scale /Nut width	24 ¾" / 1 11/16"
Fingerboard/Inlay	Ebony, 22 fret / Parallelogram
Binding	Body / Neck
Bridge/Tailpiece	Tune-o-matic/ Trapeze
Materials	Solid carved spruce top. Laminated maple sides and back. One-piece mahogany neck.
Finish	Ebony, Natural, Vintage Sunburst, Wine Red

Wes Montgomery *Vintage Sunburst*

Pickup	'57 Classic HB
Controls	One volume, one tone
Hardware	Gold
Scale /Nut width	25 ½" / 1 11/16"
Fingerboard/Inlay	Ebony, 20 fret / Block
Binding	Body / Neck / Peghead
Bridge/Tailpiece	Ebony / 24k gold with engraved Wes Montgomery silver insert
Materials	Solid carved spruce top. Solid maple sides and back. Five -piece rock maple neck.
Finish	Ebony, Vintage Sunburst, Wine Red

L5 entries from the Historic Collection catalog

Roland Prince with Norlin L5CESN

Tuck Andress insert from Hot Licks video cover

Close-up of L5CESN from Norlin's 1978 UK catalog

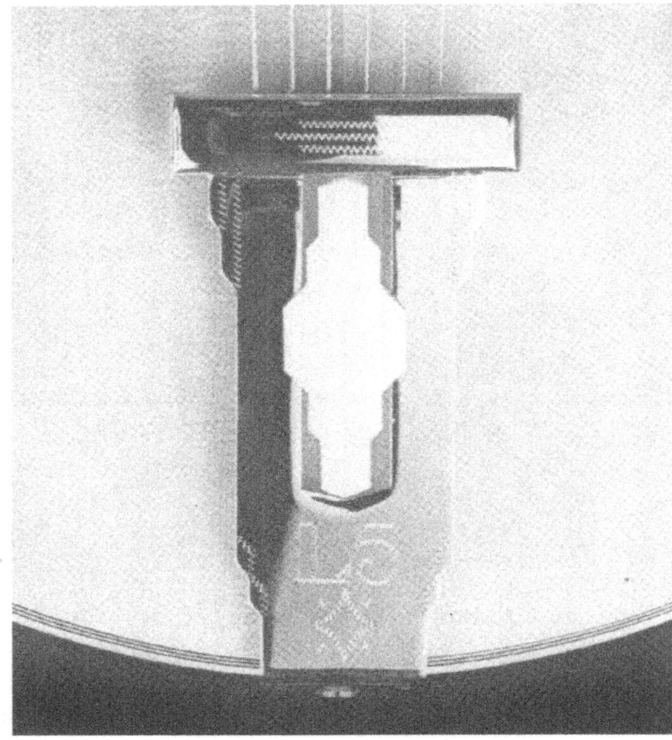

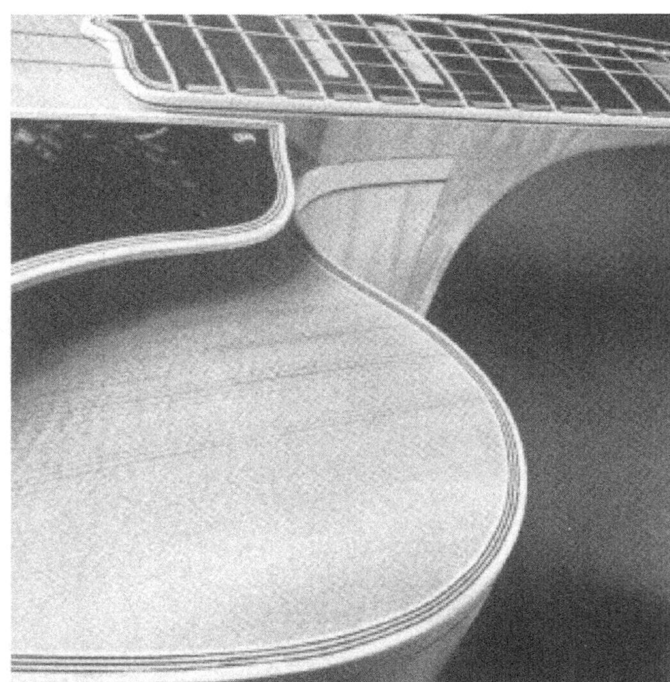

Norlin L5CN as seen from retailers file

WES
MONTGOMERY
ARTIST
TRANSCRIPTIONS
FOR GUITAR

WES MONTGOMERY
BY
ADRIAN INGRAM

POPULAR
Jazz Artist
HERB ELLIS
and his
Gibson
Herb Ellis, fabulous guitarist, whose virtuosity in combo jazz interplay is unchallenged, strums his exciting rhythms on a Gibson exclusively. Both Herb and his trio are consistent poll winners . . . heard on the air, at concerts, night clubs and on Verve label recordings.
GIBSON, INC., Kalamazoo, Michigan

CLINT STRONG
MASTERING JAZZ LICKS
REH VIDEO

Ike Issacs insert from JAZZ GUITAR SCHOOL

LOU BONNIE
Waring's Pennsylvanians

ONLY A
Gibson
IS GOOD ENOUGH

FRANK VICTOR
Radio
New York

From a Solid Block of One Inch Mountain Spruce to a Gibson Carved Top

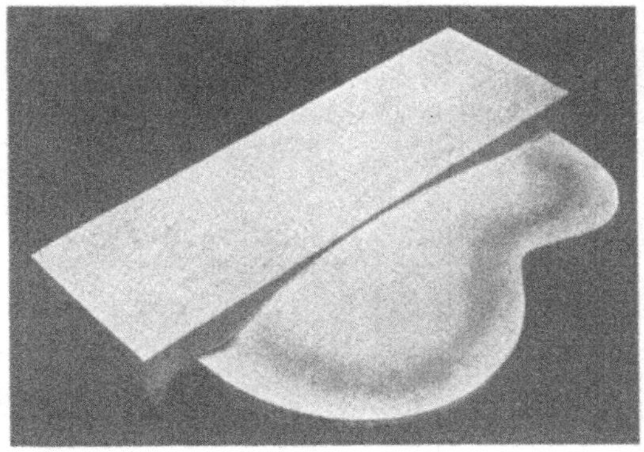

Let's follow a Gibson carved top through the hands of many experienced workmen.

After thorough open air seasoning, the fine grained, white spruce is sawed to blocks 1" thick by 18" wide by 25" long—then it is carved to rough shape by a special machine which follows a master pattern to the thousandth of an inch—this operation is supervised by a workman with over a quarter century of experience in making carved tops and backs. If the slightest flaw appears during the carving process, the top is instantly thrown out.

Now the top is ready for the most delicate of all work—the hand graduating, which can only be done by workmen with years and years of experience. After the top comes from the carving

(Continued on page 19)

[18]

TONY OLIVER
Vincent Lopez Orchestra

ONLY A
Gibson
IS GOOD ENOUGH

TED POWELL
Abe Lyman Orchestra

DICK MORGAN
Horace Heidt Orchestra

ONLY A
Gibson
IS GOOD ENOUGH

GLEN GRAY and
JACK BLANCHETTE
Casa Loma Orchestra

Just a Rod in the Neck is Not Enough --- Only Gibson has the Rod Plus Adjustment

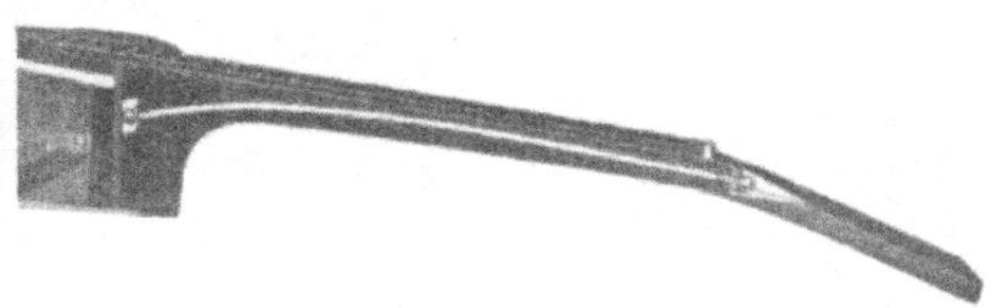

Like the carved top, Gibson originated the means of strengthening necks of guitars, banjos and mandolins with a steel rod—there is no better proof of the value of this feature than the fact that efforts have been made to copy the idea in many modern instruments.

BUT—the rod in the neck alone is not enough!

IT IS THE ADJUSTMENT THAT COUNTS—and only Gibson has it!

It is impossible to absolutely guarantee that a neck will not bend from climatic changes or the tremendous tension of the strings—and if the neck on your instrument does bend, you have wasted your money (unless it is a Gibson) because it is of no use, due to the fact that the strings are hard to push down to the fingerboard and it is out of tune in the upper registers. However—if your instrument is a Gibson, the neck can be adjusted perfectly in a few seconds, thanks to the Gibson adjustable truss rod neck construction, and you will not have to spend your money over again for a new instrument, or struggle along with sore fingers and an inaccurate instrument.

Another thing—just an ordinary straight rod in the neck does not do any good, it bends with the wood and stays bent! The Gibson truss rod is scientifically arched and braced in such a way that it continually pulls against the strain of the neck and seldom is it necessary to adjust the truss rod.

You will find the STORY OF GIBSON continued on page 14.

[10]

MUZZY MARCELLINO
Ted Fio Rito Orchestra

ONLY A
Gibson
IS GOOD ENOUGH

FRANK WORRELL
C B S Staff
New York

Tony Mottola with a double pickup (Charlie Christian) L5CES

Liberace and Elvis Presley

Jack Wilkins playing a blonde L5CES

CARVED TOP

"L5"

L5C — *Regular finish* — *Acoustic*
L5CN — *Natural finish* — *Acoustic*
L5CES — *Regular finish* — *Electric*
L5CESN — *Natural finish* — *Electric*

WITH ITS VERY FAST SLIM NECK, full strong tone, and superb appearance, the L5C continues to be the first choice of leading professional artists for solo, as well as for orchestral playing. *BODY* has first quality carved spruce top, and selected curly maple back and rim. Edges bound with five-ply black and white laminated celluloid, and "*f*" holes bound with white. Tortoise-shell finished pickguard. Dimensions — 17″ wide by 21″ long and 3½″ deep at rim. *NECK*, of curly maple, has ebonised inlay strip down back. Gibson "Truss-rod" construction allows a slimmer than usual neck and provides means of adjusting action depth. Ebony fingerboard has large pearl block inlays and is bound to match the body. Pearl inlaid, black peghead. Cutaway provides easy access to the 25½″ scale length and 20 frets. "*Vari tone*" non-vibrating tailpiece in gold and silver finish, Kluson "Sealfast" machine heads and all other fittings gold-plated.

Available either for acoustic or amplified playing in Regular Cremona brown with golden sunburst or in Natural clear finish, revealing the grain of the fine woods. Electric models have the "Tune-o-matic" bridge, two built-in pickups with separate tone and volume controls and a toggle selector switch.

TONY BRADAN

Case — #600 Faultless, plush lined
Zipper cover for this case — #ZC-6

3

1956 catalog

1959 catalog

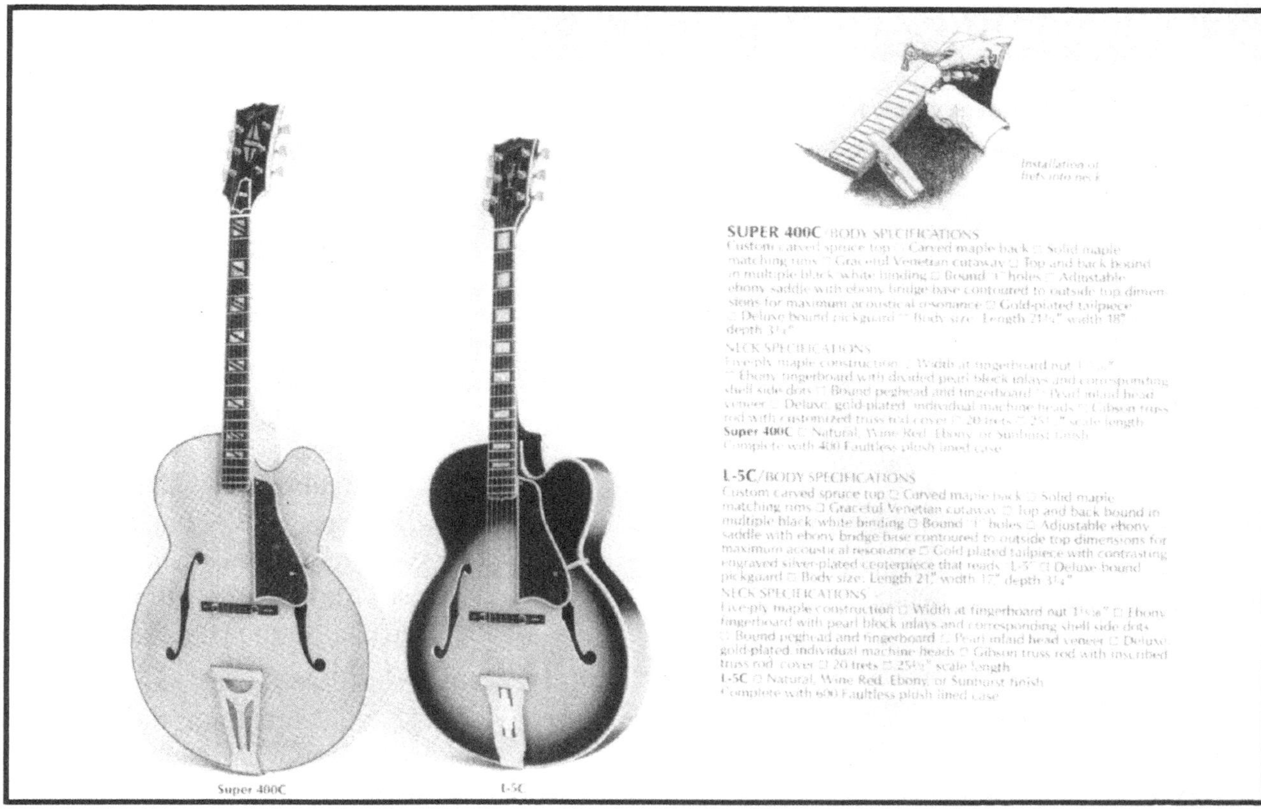

Installation of frets into neck

SUPER 400C/BODY SPECIFICATIONS
Custom carved spruce top ☐ Carved maple back ☐ Solid maple matching rims ☐ Graceful Venetian cutaway ☐ Top and back bound in multiple black/white binding ☐ Bound "f" holes ☐ Adjustable ebony saddle with ebony bridge base contoured to outside top dimensions for maximum acoustical resonance ☐ Gold-plated tailpiece ☐ Deluxe bound pickguard ☐ Body size: Length 21¾" width 18" depth 3¼"

NECK SPECIFICATIONS
Five-ply maple construction ☐ Width at fingerboard nut [illegible] ☐ Ebony fingerboard with divided pearl block inlays and corresponding shell side dots ☐ Bound peghead and fingerboard ☐ Pearl inlaid head veneer ☐ Deluxe, gold-plated, individual machine heads ☐ Gibson truss rod with customized truss rod cover ☐ 20 frets ☐ 25½" scale length
Super 400C ☐ Natural, Wine Red, Ebony, or Sunburst finish
Complete with 400 Faultless plush lined case

L-5C/BODY SPECIFICATIONS
Custom carved spruce top ☐ Carved maple back ☐ Solid maple matching rims ☐ Graceful Venetian cutaway ☐ Top and back bound in multiple black/white binding ☐ Bound "f" holes ☐ Adjustable ebony saddle with ebony bridge base contoured to outside top dimensions for maximum acoustical resonance ☐ Gold plated tailpiece with contrasting engraved silver-plated centerpiece that reads "L-5" ☐ Deluxe bound pickguard ☐ Body size: Length 21" width 17" depth 3¼"

NECK SPECIFICATIONS
Five-ply maple construction ☐ Width at fingerboard nut [illegible] ☐ Ebony fingerboard with pearl block inlays and corresponding shell side dots ☐ Bound peghead and fingerboard ☐ Pearl inlaid head veneer ☐ Deluxe gold-plated, individual machine heads ☐ Gibson truss rod with inscribed truss rod cover ☐ 20 frets ☐ 25½" scale length
L-5C ☐ Natural, Wine Red, Ebony, or Sunburst finish
Complete with 600 Faultless plush lined case

Super 400C L-5C

1970's catalog showing Super 400 and L5C

Shaping and neck carving

SUPER 400CES/BODY SPECIFICATIONS
Custom carved spruce top ☐ Carved maple back ☐ Solid maple matching rims ☐ Graceful Venetian cutaway ☐ Top and back bound in multiple black/white binding ☐ Bound "f" holes ☐ Adjustable ebony saddle with ebony bridge base contoured to outside top dimensions for maximum acoustical resonance ☐ Gold-plated tailpiece ☐ Deluxe bound pickguard ☐ Two gold-plated, Gibson Humbucking pickups with individual volume and tone controls ☐ 3-position toggle switch for pickup selection (individual or both pickups simultaneously) ☐ Body size: Length 21¾" width 18" depth 3¼"

NECK SPECIFICATIONS
Five-ply maple construction ☐ Width at fingerboard nut [illegible] ☐ Ebony fingerboard with divided pearl block inlays and corresponding shell side dots ☐ Bound peghead and fingerboard ☐ Pearl inlaid head veneer ☐ Deluxe, gold-plated, individual machine heads ☐ Gibson truss rod with customized truss rod cover ☐ 20 frets ☐ 25½" scale length
Super 400CES ☐ Natural, Wine Red, Ebony, or Sunburst finish
Complete with 400 Faultless plush lined case

L-5CES/BODY SPECIFICATIONS
Custom carved spruce top ☐ Carved maple back ☐ Solid maple matching rims ☐ Graceful Venetian cutaway ☐ Top and back bound in multiple black/white binding ☐ Bound "f" holes ☐ Adjustable ebony saddle with ebony bridge base contoured to outside top dimensions for maximum acoustical resonance ☐ Gold-plated tailpiece with contrasting engraved silver-plated centerpiece that reads "L-5" ☐ Deluxe bound pickguard ☐ Two Gibson Humbucking pickups with individual volume and tone controls ☐ 3-position toggle switch for pickup selection (individual or both pickups simultaneously) ☐ Body size: Length 21" width 17" depth 3¼"

NECK SPECIFICATIONS
Five-ply maple constuction ☐ Width at fingerboard nut [illegible] ☐ Ebony fingerboard with pearl block inlays and corresponding shell side dots ☐ Bound peghead and fingerboard ☐ Pearl inlaid head veneer ☐ Deluxe, gold-plated, individual machine heads ☐ Gibson truss rod with inscribed truss rod cover ☐ 20 frets ☐ 25½" scale length
L-5CES ☐ Natural, Wine Red, Ebony, or Sunburst finish
Complete with 600 Faultless plush lined case

Super 400CES L-5CES

1970's catalog showing Super 400CES and L5CES

APPENDIX B: *L5 CHRONOLOGY* From 1895 to 1994

1895 Orville Gibson applies for a patent on the design of carved top mandolins and guitars.

1898 Carved top patent granted.

1902 "Gibson Mandolin-Guitar Company" incorporated.

1908 Elevated pickguards and moveable bridges introduced.

1909 Elevated pickguard patented.

1910 Metal tailpiece patented.

1911 Pickguard side-fitting clamp, the basis for the L5's foot and riser block, patented. Art Nouveau flowerpot peghead inlay first used (on F4 mandolin).

1919 Lloyd Loar joins Gibson's staff.

1921 Height adjustable bridge introduced. Thaddeus McHugh patents adjustable truss rod.

1922 Master Style 5 "F" hole guitar and Adjustable truss rod introduced.

1925 Loar leaves Gibson and the last batch of Lloyd Loar signed L5 mastertone labels were produced.

1924 The L5's Virzi tone-producer was abandoned.

1927 L5's ebony fingerboard gained an additional position marker (3rd fret).

1929 The decorative point at the end of the fingerboard was phased out.

1930 Block Position Markers replaced the simple dots used to date.

1934 Advanced 17" bodies were introduced and the decorative point at the end of the fingerboard reinstated. X bracing replaced the earlier parallel method to support the larger tops.

1935 The company logo on the peghead changed from "The Gibson" to "Gibson".

1937 The Fancy art deco tailpiece was first used. Scale length increased to 25 1/2

1939 L5s internal bracing changed from X bracing back to parallel bracing to support the carved spruce top. L5P (cutaway) introduced. Additional position markers at frets 1 and 17. Natural finish option now available.

1939/40 "Varitone" tension adjuster added to the L5's art deco tailpiece. Kluson "sealfast" tuners replaced Grovers.

1942-4 L5 production virtually ceases due to wartime material shortages.

1944 Gibson acquired by Chicago Musical Instruments (C M I). Maurice Berlin becomes Secretary and Treasurer–Guy Hart remains general manager.

1947 Manufacture of L5s fully reinstated. Julius Bellson introduced the "A" prefix serial numbering system.

1951 L5CES with P90 pickups introduced.

1953/4 Tune-o-matic bridge used on CES models.

1954 Alnico "V" pickups replaced P90s.1955 Gold bonnet knobs replace larger barrel type.

1955 Four experimental L5 CES "Ts" made as prototype for the Byrdland.

1956 Tulip shaped tuning peg buttons change from plastic to metal (gold plated).

1957 PAF humbucking pickups replace Alnico "Vs".

1958 Cushioning rubber grommet added to pick-up selector switch. First L5CT shipped.

1959 L5CT officially added to the line.

1960 Florentine cutaway used for the great majority of CES models. Gold caps added to tone and volume controls. Six L5CT - Crests shipped.

1961/2 One piece laminated backs replaced two piece carved backs on the majority of CES models. L5CT "officially" discontinued apart from custom orders.

1962 Three piece laminated necks replace two piece necks on both L5C and L5CES models. L5CT "officially" discontinued apart from custom order One custom order L5C with Florentine cutaway shipped (serial No. 50043)

1963 Majority of L5CES' no longer fitted with humbuckers carrying the PAF decal.

1965 Peghead angle changes from 17 degrees to 14 degrees. Gibson make 2 custom single pickup L5CES' for Wes Montgomery.

1966 Sombrero knobs replace gold capped bonnet knobs.

1969 Florentine cutaway phased out on all CES models. Two-piece solid back reinstated. One custom order Cherry L5CT shipped

1970 C M I sells Gibson to Norlin. Oval orange label replaced by Norlin's black, white and purple rectangular label. Volutes first appear and some L5s have "Made in USA' stamp on back of headstock. Wide rimmed truss rod cover changed for a plainer version engraved: CUSTOM L-5.

1973 L5S officially launched and shipped.

1974 Nashville plant opens.

1975/6 Cherry and black added to the regular color options.

1977 Alcohol rubbing stain, "coverage" colours, antique sunburst and walnut introduced. Schaller machineheads, with retaining nut in pegs, replace regular Klusons.

1978 Super V CES and Super V/BJB introduced.

1979 Tune-o-matic bridge top on CES replaced by ebony saddle.

1980 Schaller machineheads with retractable cranks: introduced on all top of the line electrics.

1984 Kalamazoo plant closed down. All L5 models revert back to Schaller, "Kluson" copy, machineheads. Super V/BJB discontinued.

1985 Norlin sells Gibson to current owners.

1986 Limited run of 50th Anniversary L5CES'.

1988 Wooden applique with, diagonal trapezoid m.o.p. engraved "L-5", replaced the silver metal lozenge in the tailpiece.

1989 Custom Shop guitars given higher profile after the success of the Greg Rich/Jim Triggs L5 based "Las Vegas" guitar. (L5 body, Fender style peghead and diamond F holes).

1992 Prototype of Wes Montgomery L5 displayed at various shows.

1993 Gibson launches the "Historic Collection" including: 1934 L5, 1951 L5CES and WES MONTGOMERY MODELS.

1994 CENTENNIAL COLLECTION including Centennial L5CES.

APPENDIX C: *Shipping Totals*

Instrument	*1935*	*1936*	*1937*	*1938*	*1939*	*1940*	*1941*	*1948*	*1949*
L5 Small	70	6	23						
L5	30	19	251	197	152	52	51	49	29
L5N	36	38	17						
L5P	40	11	14						
L5PN	40	13							
L5C	23	23							
L5CN	21	22							

Instrument	*1950*	*1951*	*1952*	*1953*	*1954*	*1955*	*1956*	*1957*	*1958*	*1959*
L5	17	29	20	15	12	5	7	7	3	
L5N	4	11	7	1	3	8	4	2		
L5C	18	17	17	19	26	11	9	16	15	33
L5CN	23	9	15	4	13	25	11	16	3	22
L5CES	31	29	25	30	19	23	22	21	26	
L5CESN	8	17	18	20	31	32	15	27	12	
L5CT*										23

Instrument	*1960*	*1961*	*1962*	*1963*	*1964*	*1965*	*1966*	*1967*	*1968*	*1969*
L5C	26	19	21	41	23	15	25	10	36	70
L5CN	13	5	12	4	9	1	9	3	19	
L5CES	45	22	30	51	42	34	23	102	189	170
L5CESN	17	12	11	21	10	10	1	5	11	55
L5CT*	9	11								1

Instrument	*1970*	*1971*	*1972*	*1973*	*1974*	*1975*	*1976*	*1977*	*1978*	*1979*
L5C	8	10	6	2	40	34	39	13	12	
L5CN	2	2	6	1	1	4	29	23	19	3
L5CES	71	101	128	138	208	137	139	147	117	45
L5CESN	24	26	65	18	17	36	103	100	38	15
L5CESV	6	6	2	3						

Instrument	*1980*	*1981*	*1982*	*1983*	*1984*	*1985*	*1986*	*1987*	*1988*	*1989*
L5C	-	-	-	-	-	1	1	2		
L5CN	-	-	-	-	-	3				
L5CES	-	-	-	-	-	2	11	2	20	148
L5CESN	-	-	-	-	-	2	1	6	4	52

* *L5CT:George Gobel Model*

V *L5 with Super 400 Neck*

\- *No data available (1980-1984)*

APPENDIX D: *Bibliography*

Acunto, L (1994) A Look Ahead, in 20th Century Guitar Jan/Feb 1994, Vol 4 No 1, Seventh String Press, Hauppauge

Acunto, T (1994) Gibson Centennial in 20th Century Guitar, Jan/Feb 1994 Vol 4, No 1, Seventh String Press, Hauppauge

Bellson, J (1973) The Gibson Story, Gibson, Kalamazoo

Bishop, I (1979) The Gibson Guitar from 1950 Vol 1 + 2, Musical New Series, London

Carter, C (1994) Gibson Guitars–100 Years of An American Icon, G P G, Los Angeles.

Duchossoir, A (1981) Gibson Electrics, Vol I Mediapresse, Chatillion

Duchossoir, A (1983) Guitar Identification, Hal Leonard, Milwaukee

Duchossoir, A (1994) Gibson Electrics The Classic Years, Hal Leonard, Milwaukee

Gibson Corporation (1900-1995) Catalogues, Pamphlets and Flyers, Kalamazoo and Nashville.

Gladwell, R (1994) 100 Not Out, in Guitarist Sept, 1994 Vol II No 4 Guitarist Pub. Ely

Gladwell, R (1994) 100 Not Out Part II, in Guitarist Sept, 1994 Vol II No 4 Guitarist Pub. Ely

Gruhn, G (1994) Gibson A Master of Diversity, in 20th Century Guitar, Jan/Feb 1994 Vol 4 No 1 Seventh String Press, Hauppauge

Gruhn, G (1994) Gibson Celebrates 100 Years; in Vintage Guitar, Oct 1994, Vol 9, No 1, Vintage Guitar Inc., Bismark

Gruhn, G + Carter, W (1991) Gruhn Guide to Vintage Guitars, Miller Freeman, San Fransisco

Gruhn, G + Carter, W (1993) Acoustic Guitars, G P I Books, Miller Freeman, San Fransisco

Gruhn, G + Carter, W (1994) Electric Guitars and Basses, G P I Books, Miller Freeman, San Fransisco

Gruhn, G (1996) George Gobel's 1958 L5-CT Prototype, in Gruhn Guitars Monthly, Feb 1996, Nashville

Gruhn, G (1996) The Ten Most Influential American Made Acoustic Guitar Designs, in Vintage Guitar, April, Vol 10, No 7, Bismark

Ingram A (1985) Choosing An Instrument: Gibson Jazz Guitars, in "Guitarist" Vol 2 No 4 Guitarist Pub. Ely

Ingram, A (1993) The Gibson Historical Collection, in 20th Century Guitar Jan/Feb 1993, Hauppauge

Ingram A, (1994) The Art of the Archtop Guitar in "Acoustic Musician", Vol 1 No 9 Dec. 1994, Newmarket V A

Ingram A (1994) The Gibson ES175, It's History and Players, Music Maker Publications, Ely

Ingram A +Shaw D (1995) The Historic Collection, A tour of the Gibson Factory, Nashville, in "String Jazz," Edition 1, Vol 1 Jan/Feb, String Jazz Pub. Doncaster.

Ingram A (1996) Jazz Guitar Greats: Hank Garland, in Just Jazz Guitar No. 7 May, 1996

Jay, S &Wexer, L (1991) L5 Premiere–Gibson's First Cutaway Archtop in 20th Century Guitar July/August 1991, Vol 2 No 4, Seventh String Press, Hauppauge

Jay, S + Wexer, L (1994) Folk Loar in 20th Century Guitar, Jan/Feb 1994, Vol 4 No 1, Seventh String Press, Hauppauge

Kienzle, R (1981) Hank Garland, in Guitar Player, January 1981 GPI Publication Cupertino

Nelson, A (1992) George Gobel and the Gibson L5CT, in 20th Century Guitar, July/August, Hauppauge

Obrecht, J (1980) Pro's Reply, in Guitar Player, April 1980, G P I Publications

Southern, J (1996) The Gibson Custom Shop, in "Vintage Guitar" May, Vol 10, No 8 Bismark

Sprung, J (1993) Close up–The Gibson Advanced L5, in 20th Century Guitar, 1993, Hauppauge

Sprung, J (1994) Close up–Gibson Gobel L5CT in 20th Century Guitar, 1994, Hauppauge

Teagle, J (1994) Gibson: A Chronology, in 20th Century Guitar, Jan/Feb 1994, Vol 4 No 1, Seventh String Press, Hauppauge

Van Hoose, T (1983) The Gibson L5 Guitar–Guitar Trader's Vintage Guitar Bulletin, Aug 1983

Van Hoose, T (1983) The Gibson L5 Electric Models, Guitar Trader's Vintage Bulletin, Sept. 1983

Van Hoose, T (1990) Gibson Super 400CES and L5CES - The Last of Kalamazoo's Finest, in 20th Century Guitar, July/August 1990 Vol 1 No 1 Hauppauge

Van Hoose, T (1991) The Gibson Super 400 - Art of the Fine Guitar, G P I Books, Miller Freeman, San Francisco

Van Hoose, T (1994) Gibson's Role in the Development of the Carved Top Guitar, in 20th Century Guitar Jan/Feb 1994, Vol 4 No 1, Seventh String Press, Hauppauge

Vey, K (1994) Gibson L5CES and L5C, in Vintage Guitar Classics, No 2 Summer 1994, Vintage Guitar Inc., Bismark

Wheeler, T (1980) Rare Bird, in Guitar Player, June 1980, G P I Publications, Cupertino

Wheeler, T (1990) American Guitars, Harper Collins, New York

ABOUT THE AUTHOR

Adrian Ingram has been a highly respected jazz and classical guitarist since 1965. He was Senior Lecturer in Jazz Guitar at the City of Leeds College of Music between 1980 and 1994 and earned the college an international reputation for jazz guiatr tuition.

Adrian has an MA in Music and an MPhil in Music Education. He studied music education with Prof John Paynter OBE (York University) and the guitar with Barney Kessel and Howard Roberts. He was elected a Fellow of the Royal Society of Arts (FRSA) in 1987 for outstanding contribution to music education.

His international reputation as a player and teacher has been strengthened by clinics and workshops at major festivals (New York, Arlington, Cork, Llangollen, Wigan, Wirral, Hull etc.). Adrian also performs with leading jazz musicians and has made a variety of recordings on CD, LP and cassette, together with a number of Radio and TV broadcasts.

He is a columnist and consultant for **Guitarist**, Music and Reviews Editor for **Just Jazz Guitar** , and a regular contributor to **Classical Guitar, 20th Century Guitar**, **Vintage Guitar Classics** and **Vintage Guitar**.